MW00580741

Praise for Dr. Hubbard's work:

"...the very best workshop I have attended on diversity. This is world class!"

—Diversity Director

"Dr. Hubbard's book provides a unique approach to aligning Diversity Initiatives with your critical business initiatives. Full of practical tools, complex yet easy to grasp methodologies, this book presents a framework aimed at ensuring targeted, measurable outcomes."

— Je A'nna McCardie

"Dr. Hubbard has written a practical, straight-forward book which provides a roadmap to help people manage and measure diversity performance. What makes this book especially worthwhile is that he conveys his ideas in terms that line managers and senior executives will understand and that is how diversity adds value to organization performance and the bottom line."

— Emilio Egea, Vice President Human Resources
Prudential Financial

"Dr. Hubbard's measurement techniques and methodologies were instrumental in helping tie our diversity initiatives to our organization's business objectives and strategies."

—Diversity Office Leader

Diversity Training ROI

How to Measure the
Return on Investment of
Diversity Training Initiatives

BY

Edward E. Hubbard, Ph.D.

DIVERSITY TRAINING ROI How to Measure the Return on
Investment of Diversity Training Initiatives

ISBN 1-883733-30-8

Cover and book design by Dolores J. Gillum, Kathexis Design

Global Insights Publishing
832 Garfield Drive
Petaluma, CA 94954
Office: (707) 763-8380   Fax: (435) 674-1203
Web: hubbardnhubbardinc.com
Products Web: hubbardscupboard.meridian1.net

Global
Insights
Publishing

Diversity Training ROI

How to Measure the
Return on Investment of
Diversity Training Initiatives

BY

Edward E. Hubbard, Ph.D.

CONTENTS AT A GLANCE

FIGURES, TABLES, AND ILLUSTRATIONS

Preface

The link between people and profits is clear. Utilizing human capital assets is the primary vehicle to drive corporate and organizational performance and results. Thus, in a diverse world, developing diversity competent employees using a learning culture is vital for long-term success. Performance and profits are closely linked and require a comprehensive business and diversity training strategy to utilize human capital assets effectively.

Over the last several years and millions of employees trained, diversity training has come under attack in the press, on radio shows, and inside organizations as having no real evidence of its value on the financial bottom-line. Many have called it a waste of time and resources. They have used article headings such as "Diversity's Business Case Doesn't Add Up" (Hansen, Workforce. com, 2009), "Value of Diversity Training Tough to Measure," (NPR Radio, NPR.org), "Who's Still Biased?" (Bennett, Boston Globe, 2010") However, there is a wealth of concrete statistical evidence and case studies demonstrating its value and contribution. These claims are made due to the fact that few Diversity practitioners hold themselves to the professional rigor of implementing a comprehensive Instructional Systems Design (ISD) and Diversity Training Return on Investment (DTROI®) methodology for all of their diversity training initiatives.

The only way to determine that skill development and diversity training are having the desired effect is to use formal training evaluation processes and ROI-based cost-benefit analysis methods to evaluate diversity training efforts. The results of these activities can confirm the positive effects of diversity training and identify improvements to make it better. Professional Diversity training measurement and evaluation strategies can contribute to maximizing an organization's overall return on investment (ROI) or it's Return on Mission (ROM™).

This book will help you learn a diversity analytics-focused process to assess, measure, track, and report your diversity training initiatives impact to demonstrate their value in financial and other terms. Diversity training evaluation approaches used in this book are both practical and comprehensive. The process is based upon the time-honored standards of the Instructional Systems Design (ISD) methodology for professional training and development and business systems analysis technologies.

The Hubbard Diversity Training Return on Investment (DTROI®) method utilizes a comprehensive step-wise process for measuring, analyzing, interpreting and reporting your diversity training results and its impact on the organization's bottom-line. The process links strategic organizational objectives and work process flow to diversity performance and impact metrics. This book gives you step-by-step instructions, worksheets and examples to help you evaluate the impact of your diversity training initiatives in the context of organizational goals, objectives, performance, and measurable results!

Chapter One provides an overview of the Strategic Role of Evaluation in Diversity Training and its links to the organization's core business objectives and mission, while **Chapter Two** explains the detailed 7-Step Hubbard Diversity Return on Investment

(DROI®) Process model for calculating Diversity ROI in financial and other terms. **Chapter Three** meticulously guides you through the critical data collection requirements and reporting components of a Diversity Training Evaluation study. **Chapter Four** takes you step-by-step through an extensive review of the steps to perform a complete Diversity Training Needs and Requirements Analysis which generates evidence for selecting the appropriate solution (which may or may not be Diversity training). Conducting a Diversity Needs and Requirements Analysis is the cornerstone for an effective Diversity Training Return on Investment-based intervention and ROI calculation. **Chapter Five** provides comprehensive examples of Diversity Training evaluation and measurement tools. **Chapter Six** contains a detailed process to calculate the ROI value of Diversity Training. It is complete with formulas and examples to illustrate their application. **Chapter Seven** completes the book with a discussion of a five-level Diversity Measurement Taxonomy to classify and clarify the Diversity ROI operating performance levels of a Diversity Training Intervention and further define Diversity ROI Levels of Evaluation.

Acknowledgements

My first and deepest appreciation goes to my beautiful, caring wife, Myra. Your love, support, and helpful perspectives along the way always make this work possible. God and you constantly give me inspiration to continue this work in spite of the difficulties and challenges. This book is dedicated to you.

Secondly, I would like to thank my wonderful family. My mother, Geneva Hubbard whose love and strong foundation-setting values always keeps me strong. To my sisters Leona, Lois, Sylvia, Jan,Debbie, Sue, Eva, and their families as well as a host of relatives who always keep me in their prayers. To Sheila and Phillip Parks, Pearl, Pastor Shane and Tammy Wallis, and our church family at Harvest Christian Assembly and Pastor Ron and Monica Hunt and our church family at New Life Christian Fellowship as well as many others too numerous to list...Thank You.

There are a number of people, whether they know it or not, who made the completion of this book possible. Some of them provided their scholarly works. Others provided personal encouragement.

I am again indebted to the many scholars on measurement such as Drs. Jack J. and Patti Pullium Phillips, Ron Drew Stone, Susan Barksdale, Teri Lund, Sharon Fisher, Barbara Ruffino, Dr. Jac Fitz-enz, Dr. Don Kirkpatrick, researchers at ASTD, SHRM, ISPI and others too numerous to mention. Their thought-provoking research helped shape some of the major processes utilized in this framework and approach. Thank you for sharing your knowledge such that others can learn and grow.

I am particularly indebted to several diversity professionals. I would also like to thank my great colleague and friend, Emilio Egea for your terrific insights and always having my back when I need it most. I want to thank Dr. Roosevelt Thomas and all of the members of the Diversity Collegium, participants in the many Hubbard Diversity Measurement & Productivity Institute programs, particularly the "Measuring Diversity Training ROI," "Diversity Scorecard," "Diversity ROI Certification" workshops, and others too numerous to name.

To my friend, Dolores Gillum of Kathexis Design for her brilliant, creative work on this book and everything she touches. You are truly gifted and a joy to work with. You always help me get through the crunch deadlines with such grace and focus. Thank you for your friendship and hard work.

And of course, to our tremendous Hubbard & Hubbard, Inc., staff, particularly Sarah Holmberg, our outstanding operations manager, friend and kin, and Belinda Farnsworth whose support and hard work helped keep things running smoothly during this period.

In any work like this, there are many people whose contributions deserve recognition that I may have overlooked. Please forgive me if I missed you in this list. Thank you all for your guidance, love, and support.

> Dr. Edward E. Hubbard
> September, 2010
> Petaluma, California

The Strategic Role of Evaluation in Diversity Training

Introduction

The link between people and profits is clear. Utilizing human capital assets is the primary vehicle to drive organizational performance and results. Thus, in a global economy and diverse world, developing a diversity competent employee base using a learning culture is vital for long-term, national and global success. Performance and profits are closely linked and require a comprehensive diversity training strategy to utilize human capital assets effectively.

Skill development is one of several activities that must be undertaken to achieve an organization's strategic business objectives. The only way to determine that skill development and diversity training are having the desired effect is to use formal training evaluation processes as well as cost-benefit analysis methods. The results of these activities can confirm the positive effects of diversity training and development and identify improvements to make it better. Diversity training measurement and evaluation strategies can contribute to maximizing an organization's overall return on investment (ROI or return on mission (ROM™). This chapter provides an introduction to the topic of diversity training evaluation and illustrates approaches that can be used to identify the "hard" and "soft" measures of diversity training that link to the bottom-line and ROI/ ROM™.

Building a Framework for Success

Any organization that wants to succeed, and continue to succeed, has to recruit and maintain a diverse workforce consisting of people who are willing to accept change and willing to learn for continuous improvement. This is true of everyone in the workforce from the Chief Executive Officer to the newest recruit. One of the jobs of the Chief Diversity Officer (or Diversity Director) can be divided into three main parts:

▶ Defining and monitoring the diverse workforce people skills and competencies needed.

▶ Recruiting and retaining people capable of meeting or developing cultural competencies, strategic process management skills, technical and other competencies needed to leverage diversity as a ROI and performance improvement strategy; and

▶ Providing the learning opportunities and resources required for effective organizational performance.

ROM™ is a registered trademark of Hubbard & Hubbard, Inc., All Rights Reserved.

Defining and monitoring the learning needs of a diverse workforce must be a deliberate and comprehensive process. This task has been described using many terms such as manpower planning, human resource assessment, skill needs analysis, *etc.* It is not the name given to the activity that matters per se, it is the work that is done to identify the diverse workforce needs at all levels that is important. This is not a one-off exercise—it is a continuous process of assessing business needs as they constantly change, analyzing the implementation and effects of your diversity strategic plan learning interventions. As a regular practice, it is important to gauge the ROI impact on the organization's performance.

Over the last several years and millions of employees trained, diversity training has come under attack in the press, on radio shows, and inside organizations as having no real evidence of its value on the financial bottom-line. Many have called it a waste of time and resources. They have used article headings such as "Diversity's Business Case Doesn't Add Up" (Hansen, Workforce. com, 2009), "Value of Diversity Training Tough to Measure," (NPR Radio, NPR.org), "Who's Still Biased?" (Bennett, *Boston Globe*, 2010") However, there is a wealth of concrete statistical evidence and case studies demonstrating its value and contribution. These claims are made due to the fact that few Diversity practitioners hold themselves to the professional rigor of implementing a comprehensive Instructional Systems Design (ISD) and Diversity Training Return on Investment (DTROI®) methodology for all of their diversity training initiatives. (These concepts will be discussed in detail later in the book.)

I have always thought of diversity as a professional discipline

DTROI® is a registered trademark of Hubbard & Hubbard, Inc., All Rights Reserved.

and field of study. However, if it is to be taken seriously as a discipline and field of study, it must possess a structure, framework and critical components that are consistent with other serious disciplines. For example, if we examine the disciplines of Marketing, Sales, Operations, and the like, we would find they all have well-defined competencies, proven theories, and applied sciences that under gird their application. These theories and sciences provide a recognized structure, strategy and a set of measurable standards to guide those who work in the field. In the field of training and development, approaches such as Instructional Systems Design (ISD) and Diversity Training Return on Investment (DTROI®) methodologies are fundamental standards of practice if diversity professionals want to operate as a credible business partner doing quality work in a professional field of study. Diversity evaluation and Diversity Return on Investment DROI®) studies along with cost-benefit analysis must be standard operating policy and practice for effective client work. In fact, how can we convince our clients that the business need which the diversity or training initiative was supposed to address was successfully met without evaluative, ROI-based evidence that demonstrates that result?

The starting point for this assessment of needs will be the corporate strategic business plan or an agency's mission (if you work for a government, educational, or non-profit entity). In addition, management must be interviewed to ascertain how they anticipate the plan is going to be achieved and to determine organizational needs from their point of view. As the corporate strategic plan can only be achieved by people, it is obvious that a first priority is to ensure that a diverse workforce exists that possess the appropriate interpersonal and technical skills to create a competitive advantage. Therefore, a crucial first step is to define what these diverse workforce competencies and needs are. (This will be discussed this in greater detail in Chapter Four.)

I believe that training can be defined as *'helping people to learn effectively to know or perform to meet a specific set of objectives.'* This means that a primary role of diversity training is to create and provide a learning environment with the very best diversity and inclusion learning opportunities to meet an organization's specific objectives and targeted outcomes. Learning is something people choose to do when they are interested in what is happening around them. If the organization is one in which diverse people can learn, then employees will have the opportunity to develop and maintain the skills they need.

The Learning and Evaluation-focused Organization

Learning involves a constant interaction between people and their environment through experimentation, exploration, and questioning. An environment that is exciting, and one in which people have fun, leads to considerable learning and growth. Building a learning organization means encouraging people to be themselves, to question and explore their working environment. This allows them to influence what goes on around them. For this to happen changes have to take place in what I will call the conventional rule-based organization, where supervision is concerned with getting people to toe the line rather than learn and grow. To learn, people have to open their minds to new ideas and suggestions, and learn to effectively work across cultures, differences, functions, *etc.*, in a way that includes and values others, then take the time to evaluate the impact of this learning application in driving organizational performance. This is encouraged and viewed as a requirement in a learning and evaluation-focused organization.

In the learning and evaluation-focused organization, diversity and inclusion training is not an activity which is separate from day to day activities: it is an inherent part of business and part of the diverse working environment. When a person needs to know something, or wants to learn something, the information and the support systems to learn should be immediately available to them. Sometimes this can be done while the work activity continues, and sometimes a short break may need to be taken. Where it is not possible for the work activity to be interrupted people should be able to access competency training for diverse workforce effectiveness as soon as they can. Employees should be encouraged to take the time and make the effort to learn. This encouragement should come from colleagues, supervisors, and management.

If the organization is truly a learning organization, it is willing to learn from diverse customers and suppliers, from competitors, from the market place, and from its workforce. In this way change is not only accepted, it is eagerly sought out, and the challenge it brings is welcomed. This reduces the resistance to change and strengthens the organization's ability to be flexible.

A learning and evaluation-focused culture grows from practice and example. When senior management act in a way which shows the people who work for them that they embrace and value diversity and inclusion and are willing to listen and learn, then people will model their own attitudes accordingly. It demonstrates that they believe in constant and continuous attention to the learning needs of others. There is no way that a new approach can be 'announced' with the expectation that it will be completely successful on its own. It has to be integrated into the fabric and the way the organization does business. It must be introduced slowly and modeled carefully, starting with the chief executive and other critical staff.

Performance and Profits

As stated earlier, the link between the performance of people and profits is generally accepted as being obvious. However, when individuals are asked how their performance impacts on profits they are often hard pressed to produce a direct link. The link can be established for every member of the diverse workforce if measured and evaluated using a comprehensive analytics strategy. Once this link is established, it is possible to measure and demonstrate how improved diversity performance will increase profit. Examples demonstrating this link will be highlighted in case studies throughout this book.

If improved performance comes from the growth and development of individual skills and competencies that are utilized to address strategic business issues, then a direct link can be made between diversity training and profits. Helping people to learn strategic diversity competencies and skills that affect its marketplace is directly helping to improve organizational performance, and hence profits. In some cases however, investment made in diversity training may not have an immediate payoff. But few investments have. By measuring the returns from diversity and inclusion training in terms of performance improvement, it is possible to prepare a financial investment analysis or "DROI® study" for diversity training initiatives that show tangible, financial results This provides management with a clear indication of the value of the diversity training investment and helps to convince everyone that diversity and inclusion training is a valuable investment in people and profits.

Investing in the Future

The future success of an organization's business is forged in what it does today. It is forged on the anvil of experience by the craft of professionals such as skilled diversity professionals and other strategic business partners. When a learning organization is in full operation, everything that diverse workforce members do should lead them to learn something about themselves, how effectively they are doing it, and its impact on the objectives, outcomes and results of the organization.

Learning opportunities should be sought out by everyone. To learn about people who are different than themselves, employees should be encouraged to explore areas across differences that interest them, and to grow and develop as people. This may be irrespective of their learning having an immediate connection with the work they are doing. This will help lay a firm foundation for skills needed to operate in a diverse work environment and marketplace both now and in the future.

It is not always easy for some organizations to provide support for initiatives that are not 'job' related. There seems to be an attitude that only learning directly concerned with the 'job' is valid, and that any other learning is inappropriate, as if diversity and inclusion training is "not job related." This attitude is very backward thinking. When management is thinking about the future they cannot possibly know what individuals will aspire to do or what future competitive business requirements will demand in a global marketplace, so they cannot assume that current learning is not valid for the future simply because it doesn't relate to the 'current job'. If management is truly concerned to equip the workforce for the future then they have to take a forward-looking attitude, and support and encourage employees to learn the things they aspire to as well as learning those things that link in with the organization's strategic plan and mission. Given what we know about organizational functioning and our changing U.S. and global diversity, it is a pretty safe bet that having diversity and inclusion competencies and skills will be a valuable asset.

Evaluating Strategies for Success

Success is measured in a wide variety of ways. Corporate success in diverse markets, for example, is usually measured on the basis of profitability, but there are always other factors involved such as high quality, efficient and friendly service, and so on. Individuals measure success differently. Some clearly measure success in terms of their income, and display their success through status symbols. Others measure success in terms of personal achievement, *e.g.* learning to speak another language, being able to make good presentations, being elected as chairperson of an employee resource group, and so on. Therefore, when developing strategies for success it is first necessary to decide what constitutes success. For example, success statements might consist of the following: "We will consider ourselves successful if we earn a profit per person of $50,000, or if we see a reduction in the number of diverse customer complaints decrease to less than 100 per year," or if "our accident-free operating days reach the 2000 target," or "if we all achieve our personal success statements defined at the beginning of the year to become culturally competent and capable."

The organization can issue regular updates regarding how close it is to these success targets. At the individual level everyone should prepare their own core competency success statement, which is agreed to with their manager, and which is used as a basis for measuring progress. It is valuable if personal success statements include some items that relate to improving their individual performance as a diverse work team member, and helping achieve corporate success objectives. Once this approach is in place it becomes possible to determine the appropriate diversity training-related strategies required to meet both personal and corporate level objectives.

If every member of the diverse workforce is interested in and committed to personal performance and achieving their own success objectives, then there is every chance that the corporate objectives can be achieved. Setting corporate targets without every individual knowing how they can contribute is doomed to failure. Corporate success depends upon individual success. Individual success depends upon the motivation and skill-based development support they receive to learn, to grow, and to improve their performance. To do this successfully, employees and the organization must be kept informed with goal-oriented and competency-based evaluative feedback that the behavioral changes generated by diversity training are being applied and integrated into the way the organization does its business. And, that the utilization of these diversity-related competencies and approaches has produced strategic performance benefits and DROI®/DROM™.

If diversity training and evaluation is to play a strategic role in producing an organization's results, it must be utilized as a comprehensive business strategy that is tied to the organizational mission and vision. It should not be treated as merely a program or process with no performance-related value. It must be monitored, measured, and utilized as part of the organization's competitive arsenal to meet business and organizational challenges head-on! This book will show you how.

References

"Diversity's Business Case Doesn't Add Up" (Fay Hansen, Workforce.com, February, 2009)

"Value of Diversity Training Tough to Measure," (NPR Radio, Talk of the Nation, March 9, 2010, NEAL CONAN, host: NPR.org),

"Who's Still Biased?", Drake Bennett, *Boston Globe*, March, 2010"

Hubbard, Edward E., *How to Calculate Diversity Return on Investment*. California: Global Insights Publishing, 1999.

Hubbard, Edward E., *The Diversity Scorecard: Evaluating the Impact of Diversity on Organizational Performance*. Massachusetts: Butterworth-Heinemann, Elsevier Publishing, 2004.

Hubbard, Edward E., *The Diversity Discipline: Implementing Diversity Work with a Strategy, Structure, and ROI Measurement Focus*. California: Global Insights Publishing, 2009.

Jackson, Susan E., *Diversity in the Workplace*. New York: The Guilford Press, 1992.

Plummer, Deborah L., *Handbook of Diversity Management*. Maryland: University Press of America, Inc. 2003

CHAPTER 2

The Diversity Return on Investment (DROI) Process

Introduction

Interest in diversity and the return-on-investment associated with it is increasing. Several issues such as changing national workforce demographics and the global economy are driving this increased interest and its application to a wide range of related issues. Pressures from senior managers, Boards of Directors, stockholders, and clients to show the return on diversity investment is probably the most influential driver. Competitive economic pressures are causing intense scrutiny of all expenditures, including all diversity costs. In addition, diversity professionals know they must begin to show how diversity is linked to the bottom line in hard numbers. In short, they must calculate and report their diversity ROI like any other part of the business.

DROI: A Systematic Approach to Measurement

Calculating Diversity Return on Investment (DROI) requires asking key questions and performing key tasks along the way. To achieve a successful result, measuring DROI® requires a systematic approach that takes into account both costs and benefits. The Hubbard Diversity ROI Analysis Model, as shown below, provides a step-by-step approach that keeps the process manageable so users can tackle one issue at a time (Hubbard, 1999).

Hubbard Diversity ROI Analysis Model.

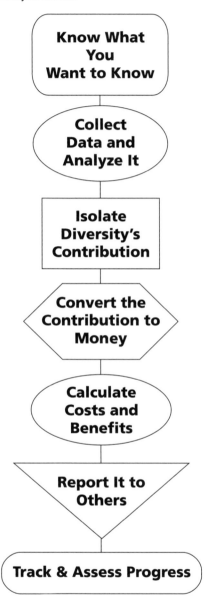

Source: *How to Calculate Diversity Return on Investment (DROI)*, by Dr. Edward E. Hubbard, 1999, 2004

The model also emphasizes that this logical, systematic process flows from one step to another. Applying the model provides consistency from one DROI® calculation to another. In essence, it suggests that the major aspects of diversity measurement you need to address include the following:

▶ Initial analysis and planning

▶ Collecting and analyzing data

▶ Isolating diversity's contribution

▶ Converting the contribution to money

▶ Calculating the costs and benefits

▶ Reporting data

▶ Tracking and assessing progress

Step 1: Initial Analysis and Planning

Creating an effective DROI-based training evaluation analysis process requires that you clearly identify what you want to know as a result of implementing a diversity training measurement study. This should be based on, at bare minimum, the identification of business problems or opportunities related to the organization's key business strategy and/or the Diversity Needs Analysis outcomes you generated during the Diversity Training Needs Analysis phase. You should also be prepared to list a series of research questions you would like answered or hypotheses you would like to test. These questions may include things such as "In what racial categories do we have the highest level of diversity-competent employees?", "In what diverse customer markets have we trained our sales force to utilize cultural competencies and multicultural marketing strategies to sell our products or services and enhance our ROI?", or "How has our diverse work team innovation strategies workshop improved operational performance and the idea- and solution-generation (creative) process using current cross-functional teams?"

While planning ways to address these research questions and ideas, it may be helpful to begin with the end in mind. That is, think of what will appear on your research report that will ultimately become an outcome that drives your ***Diversity Training Return on Investment (DTROI®) Report,*** create placeholders for them, and then generate the questions or hypotheses that must be answered in order for data to show up on the report as results. The final step in this phase is to summarize the questions you would like answered and formulate diversity measurement study objectives that will guide your work. Once this is done, you are ready to consider the appropriate data collection methods and develop your data collection plan.

Step 2: Collecting and Analyzing Data

Data collection is central to the DROI® process. A good portion of your data will be collected using the "in-class" and "end-of-class" training evaluation methods. In some situations, post-DROI study data are collected and compared to pre-study situations, control group differences, and expectations. Both hard data (representing output, quality, cost, time, and frequency) and soft data (including work habits, work climate, and attitudes) are collected. Data are collected using a variety of methods, including but not limited to the following:

▶ Follow-up surveys

▶ Post-study interviews

▶ Focus groups

▶ Short-term pilot project assignments

▶ Action plans

▶ Performance contracts (agreements to produce certain levels of results)

▶ Performance monitoring (reports and other literature reviews)

The important challenge in the data collection phase is to select the method or methods appropriate for the organizational setting and within the time and budget constraints of the organization. During this phase, you will identify the data collection processes and specific metrics to use, create the appropriate evaluation instruments, and apply an organizational change methodology such as the Hubbard Diversity 9-S Framework, which includes Shared Vision, Shared Values, Standards, Strategy, Structure, Systems, Style, Skills, and Staff Diversity (Hubbard, 1999).

Step 3: Isolating Diversity's Contribution

An often-overlooked issue in most diversity training assessments or evaluation studies is the process of isolating the effects of the diversity intervention. In this step of the process, specific strategies are explored that determine the amount of output performance directly related to the diversity training initiative. This step is essential because many factors will influence performance data after the diversity training initiative as illustrated in below

Figure 2-1   Source: adapted from Jack J. and Patti P. Phillips, ROI Fieldbook.

DIVERSITY TRAINING SOLUTION

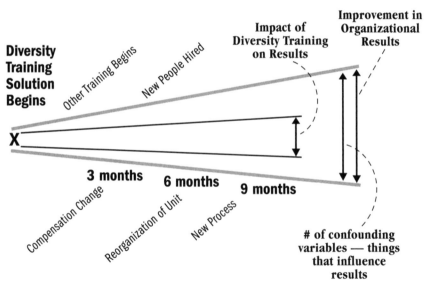

The result is increased accuracy and credibility of the DROI® calculation. The following strategies have been utilized by organizations to tackle this important issue:

- ▶ Control groups

- ▶ Trend lines

- ▶ Forecasting model

- ▶ Participant estimates

- ▶ Supervisor of participant estimates

- ▶ Senior management estimates

- ▶ Expert estimates

- ▶ Subordinate's estimates (those who work for the participants)

- ▶ Identifying other influencing factors

- ▶ Customer inputs

Collectively, these strategies provide a comprehensive set of tools to tackle the important and critical issue of isolating the effects of diversity initiatives. Calculating and isolating DROI® will require an analysis of operational and other business processes to isolate the specific areas where diversity training can be applied to improve business performance. One tool to analyze operational processes is the S-I-P-O-C Chain. This analysis tool allows you to break down operational processes and view them in terms of the way business is done from supplier to input to process to output to customer. Once all contributing factors have been identified and their contributions calculated, you would be ready to convert the contribution to money.

Step 4: Converting the Contribution to Money

To calculate the DROI® of Diversity Training, data collected in a DROI® evaluation study are converted to monetary values and are compared to the diversity initiative costs. This requires a value to be placed on each unit of data connected with the initiative. There are at least 10 different strategies available to convert data to monetary values. The specific strategy selected usually depends on the type of data and the initiative under analysis (Phillips, 2001):

1. **Output data** are converted to profit contribution or cost saving. In this strategy, output increases are converted to monetary value based on their unit contribution to profit or the unit of cost reduction.

2. The **cost of quality** is calculated and quality improvements are directly converted to cost savings.

3. For diversity initiatives where employee time is saved, the **participant's wages and benefits** are used for the value of time. Because a variety of programs focus on improving the time required to complete projects, processes, or daily activities, the value of time becomes an important and critical issue.

4. **Historical costs** are used when they are available for a specific variable. In this case, organizational cost data are utilized to establish the specific value of an improvement.

5. When available, **internal and external experts** may be used to estimate a value for an improvement. In this

situation, the credibility of the estimate hinges on the expertise and reputation of the individual.

6. **External databases** are sometimes available to estimate the value or cost of data items. Research, government, and industry databases can provide important information for these values. The difficulty lies in finding a specific database related to the diversity initiative under analysis.

7. **Participants** estimate the value of the data item. For this approach to be effective, participants must be capable of providing a value for the improvement.

8. **Supervisors of participants** provide estimates when they are both willing and capable of assigning values to the improvement. This approach is especially useful when participants are not fully capable of providing this input or in situations where supervisors need to confirm or adjust the participant's estimate.

9. **Senior management** may provide estimates on the values of an improvement. This approach is particularly helpful to establish values for performance measures that are very important to senior management.

10. **Diversity staff** estimates may be used to determine the value of an output data item. In these cases, it is essential for the estimates to be provided on an unbiased basis.

Step 4 in the Hubbard DROI Analysis Model is very important and is absolutely necessary for determining the monetary benefits from a diversity initiative. The process is challenging, particularly with soft data, but it can be accomplished if done in a systematic way using one or more of these strategies.

Step 5: Calculating the Costs and Benefits

Calculating the Diversity Initiative Costs

To successfully calculate the DROI of Diversity Training initiatives, both cost and benefits must be tracked and calculated in the process. The first part of the equation in a cost/benefit analysis is the diversity initiative costs. Tabulating the costs involves monitoring or developing all of the related costs of the diversity training initiative targeted for the DROI calculation. Among the cost components that should be included are the following:

▶ The cost to design and develop the diversity initiative, possibly pro-rated over the expected life of the initiative

▶ The cost of any materials and external staff resources utilized

▶ The costs of any facilities, travel, lodging, and so on

▶ Salaries, plus employee benefits of the employees involved

▶ Administrative and overhead costs allocated in some way

Calculating the DROI

The DROI of a Diversity Training initiative is calculated using the initiative's benefits and costs. The benefit/cost ratio (BCR) is the initiative benefits divided by cost. In formula form it is:

BCR = Diversity Initiative Benefits ÷ Diversity Initiative Costs

Sometimes the ratio is stated as a cost-to-benefit ratio, although the formula is the same as BCR. The DROI% calculation uses the net benefits of the diversity initiative divided by the initiative costs. The net benefits are the diversity initiative benefits minus the costs. As a formula, it is stated as:

DROI% = (Net Diversity Initiative Benefits ÷ Diversity Initiative Costs) × 100

In other words, the DROI formula is calculated as:

$$\frac{\text{Diversity Benefits} - \text{Diversity Initiative Costs}}{\text{Initiative Cost}} \times 100$$

This is the same basic formula used in evaluating other investments where the ROI is traditionally reported as earnings divided by investment. The DROI from some diversity initiatives is often high. DROI figures above 450 percent are not uncommon (Hubbard, 1999).

Identifying Intangible Benefits

In addition to tangible, monetary benefits, most diversity initiatives will have intangible, nonmonetary benefits. The DROI calculation is based on converting both hard and soft data to monetary values. Intangible benefits include items such as the following:

- ▶ Increased job satisfaction

- ▶ Increased organizational commitment

- ▶ Improved teamwork

- ▶ Reduced conflict

- ▶ *Etc.*

During data analysis, every attempt is made to convert all data to monetary values. All hard data such as output, quality, and time are converted to monetary values. The conversion of soft data is attempted for each data item; however, if the process used for conversion is too subjective or inaccurate, the resulting values can lose credibility in the process. This data should be listed as an intangible benefit with the appropriate explanation. For some diversity initiatives, intangible, nonmonetary benefits are extremely valuable, often carrying as much influence as the hard data items.

Step 6: Reporting Data

Next, it is critical that you have an organized communications plan to let others know the progress and challenges being addressed by the diversity training initiatives. During the development cycle of the communications plan, it is important to identify communication vehicles to use, how and when the report will be created, when it will be delivered, and how to evaluate its implementation.

Step 7: Tracking and Assessing Progress

Finally, in order to maintain any gains made or benefits from lessons learned during the process, you must make plans to track and assess the effectiveness of your diversity training initiatives over time.

The Role of Diversity in Creating ROI

Building an effective diversity training measurement system requires a firm understanding of the role diversity plays in creating a return-on-investment for the organization. A diversity training measurement system lets you do two important things: (1) manage diversity training as a strategic asset and (2) demonstrate diversity's contribution and link it to your organization's strategic business and financial success. Although each organization will describe its diversity measurement process in its own way, a well-thought-out diversity training measurement system, linked to your diversity scorecard, should get you thinking about four major themes:

1. The key diversity training deliverables that will leverage diversity's role in the organization's overall strategy.

2. Developing a high-performance work environment that utilizes diversity competencies as an asset.

3. The extent to which the environment is aligned with the organization's strategy.

4. The efficiency with which those deliverables are generated.

Identifying Diversity Training Deliverables

To build an effective diversity training measurement system for any organization, we must understand the organization's strategy implementation process in detail, along with its strategic business goals, objectives, and key performance drivers. This means understanding diversity's role and the cultural competencies needed in supporting these elements as part of a larger strategy map. For example, the organization could have profitability goals focusing on *revenue growth* and *productivity improvement.* We could describe diversity training's role in this process in the following way:

Revenue growth ultimately derives from increased customer satisfaction in all market segments, which in turn is boosted by product innovation and reliable delivery schedules, among other things. Diversity training can help the organization's sales force, for example, relate to diverse customer service requirements that drive satisfaction and recurring revenue.

Product innovation strongly depends on the presence of talented staff with significant experiences. Through trained, competency-based, diversity-friendly selection methods and retention programs, diversity contributes to a *stable, high-talent staffing deliverable* that helps the organization meet its objectives.

Reliable delivery schedules in part hinge on the maintenance of optimal staffing levels. Even if turnover is low, the organization must fill vacancies quickly. By reducing the recruiting cycle time through more diverse candidate sources and diversity-related training and on-boarding approaches, diversity supports an *optimal staffing level deliverable*, which can reduce overall costs that adds to the DROI impact.

Productivity improvement has links to maintaining optimal production and process schedules, which in turn depend on maintaining appropriate staffing levels. Again, diversity assistance in driving recruiting cycle time drives staffing levels that help keep production downtime resulting from personnel issues to a minimum (Becker, Huselid, Ulrich, 2001).

Developing a High-Performance Work Environment

Once the diversity training and other deliverables have been clearly identified, we can begin to identify and measure the primary environmental components that help generate these deliverables. This high-performance work environment system is specifically designed to help drive the organization's strategy implementation process using diversity deliverables. This could involve, for example, designing, training, and implementing a valid diversity leadership competency model that is linked to major elements in the high-performance work environment system and providing regular 360-degree multi-rater feedback to these leaders regarding their use and level of competence in applying the diversity management skills trained in the classroom. As with any element of a diversity measurement system, these data can be presented in a variety of ways.

Alignment with Strategy

The next component in the diversity training measurement system should encourage you to gauge the alignment of the diversity training measurement system with the organization's strategy implementation process. To transform a generic high-performance work system into a strategic asset, you need to focus that system directly on the diverse workforce talent aspects of those drivers. The focus must be on the diversity deliverables required to create value in the organization, which in turn highlight specific elements of the diversity training measurement system that reinforce one another in order to produce those deliverables. Therefore, specific diversity training alignment measures will be linked directly to specific deliverables in the measurement system (example: training multicultural competencies to reduce transition startup and critical incident costs in opening a new offices in the BRIC countries — Brazil, Russia, India, China, as part of the organization's global expansion). Connecting them in this way highlights the cause-and-effect relationships needed to support diversity training's contribution to the organization's strategic performance and results.

To select the appropriate alignment measures, focus on those elements of your diversity training measurement system that make a definable and significant contribution to a particular organizational strategy deliverable. These will differ for each organization. Identifying these measures requires that you combine a professional understanding of diversity with a thorough knowledge of the value-creation process in your organization. Remember that these alignment measures will follow directly from a top-down approach. Based on a larger strategy map that you will create in the diversity strategic planning process, you will identify your diversity training deliverables, which in turn will point to certain elements of the DROI measurement system that require alignment. Therefore, no standard alignment measures can be provided as examples. Instead, each organization must develop a standard process by which it develops its own set of alignment measures (both internal and external) that are tied to its business and mission outcomes.

Diversity Efficiency: Core versus Strategic Measures

As you consider which organizational strategy areas align with your diversity training efforts, remember there are a wide variety of benchmarks and standards by which you can measure diversity's efficiency. Some of these measures include the following:

- ▶ Absenteeism rate by job category and job performance by group

- ▶ Number of stress-related illnesses by group

- ▶ Turnover costs

- ▶ Number of recruiting advertising programs in place by demographic group

- ▶ Average employee tenure by performance level by group

- ▶ Number of incidents of injury by group

- ▶ Time to fill an open position by group

- ▶ Offer-to-acceptance rate by group (diversity hit rate)

- ▶ Average time for dispute resolution by group

- ▶ Cost per grievance by group

- ▶ Cost per trainee-hour

- ▶ Lost time due to accidents by group

All of these measures can be affected by your diversity training intervention and encourage cost savings. They are diversity operational measures. For the most part, they only position diversity as a commodity and serve as generic benchmarks. The key is to identify those measures that help create strategic value for the organization. Of course, these will differ for each organization because each organization's strategic value will be unique. It is important to select the measures you include in your diversity training measurement system carefully. Otherwise, it is possible to become overwhelmed by all of the potential metric choices. Benchmarking is fine for diversity commodity activities, but it has no significant influence on your organization's ability to implement its strategy.

Therefore, an approach to creating your Diversity Training measurement strategy is to divide your key efficiency metrics into two categories: core and strategic. *Core efficiency measures* represent significant diversity expenditures, but they make no real direct contribution to the organization's strategy implementation. *Strategic efficiency measures* assess the efficiency of diversity activities and processes designed to produce diversity deliverables. To make the distinction between these two types of measures, you must trace the links between the specific measure and its connection with the diversity value chain. An example might be reducing the minority recruiting cycle time. Because this is one of the first steps in helping the organization achieve the strategic objective of stable staffing levels (a key performance driver), it is an enabler and essential to a key performance driver that adds value. Separating the two helps you evaluate the net benefits of strategic deliverables and guides resource-allocation decisions as well as what diversity-related training will best meet the organization's strategic outcomes.

Final Thoughts

The implementation of your Diversity Training Return on Investment (DTROI®) study and your diversity training evaluation and measurement system is critical to the success of the organization and the credibility and survival of the diversity profession. In order to be taken seriously, diversity professionals must become adept at measuring and reporting the right diversity training results that tie diversity to the organization's bottom-line objectives. These metrics must go beyond the "number of attendees attending training" and simple "smile sheet" ratings that don't meet basic training DROI Level 1 standards. By using a systematic, logical, planned approach, and the DTROI® process, diversity training represents one of the organization's best investments in improved strategic performance and ROI.

References

Becker, Brian E., Mark A. Huselid, & Dave Ulrich. *The HR Scorecard: Linking People, Strategy, and Performance*. Boston: Harvard Business School Press, 2001.

Hubbard, Edward E. *How to Calculate Diversity Return on Investment*. Petaluma, CA: Global Insights, 1999.

Hubbard, Edward E. *The Diversity Scorecard: Evaluating the Impact of Diversity on Organizational Performance*. Massachusetts: Butterworth-Heinemann, Elsevier Publishing, 2004.

Hubbard, Edward E. *The Diversity Discipline: Implementing Diversity Work with a Strategy, Structure, and ROI Measurement Focus*. California: Global Insights Publishing, 2009.

Phillips, Jack J., Ron D. Stone, & Patricia P. Phillips. *The Human Resources Scorecard*. Boston: Butterworth–Heinemann, 2001.

Further Reading

Casio, Wayne F. *Costing Human Resources: The Financial Impact of Behavior in Organizations*, 4th ed. Australia: South-Western College Publishing, 2000.

Phillips, Jack J. *Accountability in Human Resources Management*. Boston: Butterworth–Heinemann, 1996.

CHAPTER 3

Critical Requirements for Measuring Diversity Training's Impact

Introduction

Measuring the impact of diversity training requires that you have a detailed understanding of the DROI® study process and how it works. It begins with some initial planning, and continues with the implementation of a comprehensive data collection process. The initial planning and analysis step is critical for generating a successful training evaluation and/or DTROI™ study. Many practitioners trying to develop a diversity training measurement system find out after the fact that they should have spent more time planning the strategic linkage and alignment of the diversity initiatives that will drive their training outcomes. Initial analysis and planning creates several advantages and involve several key issues we will explore. The first issue is outlining what the diversity training evaluation or DTROI® study will involve and ways to determine the success of the study — in advance, in specific detail.

In this chapter, we will focus on detailed techniques for collecting data during and after a diversity training initiative. You will be introduced to a range of approaches and methods for gathering data that will help you better understand the processes that link to creating the measures that support your diversity evaluation strategy.

Diversity Training Evaluation: Project Requirements

It is important to have as much detail as possible when specifying the requirements of a Diversity Training ROI evaluation study. Many projects run into difficulty, misunderstandings and differences in expected outcomes because the requirements are not planned and well documented. These issues are often outlined in a diversity training project proposal or detailed in the project's scope documentation. Regardless of the way it is developed, the following items should be included to achieve the best chance for success. More importantly, the Diversity Training professional and the evaluation project's sponsor (the client) need to reach agreement about these key issues to create partnership and accountability for the end result.

When it comes to training evaluation projects, there are two sets of objectives. First, there are the objectives for the Diversity

Training evaluation project itself, indicating specifically what will be accomplished and delivered through the evaluation process. The other set of objectives is called the Diversity Training initiative objectives and focuses on the goals of the actual Diversity Training initiative that will ultimately add value to the organization. In this section, our focus will center on the objectives of the Diversity Training evaluation project.

Every Diversity Training evaluation project should have a major project objective and in most cases, multiple objectives. The objectives should be as specific as possible and focused directly on the Diversity Training evaluation. Sample project objectives may include the following:

- ▶ Determine if the Diversity Training initiative is accomplishing its objectives

- ▶ Identify the strengths and weaknesses in the Diversity Training initiative

- ▶ Determine the benefit/cost ratio of the Diversity Training initiative

- ▶ Identify who benefited the most and least from the Diversity Training initiative

- ▶ Gather data to assist in pursuing future initiatives

As the list illustrates, the objectives are broad in scope, outlining from an overall perspective what is to be accomplished. The details of timing, specifications, and specific deliverables come later. The broad Diversity Training evaluation project objectives are critical because they bring focus to the project quickly. They define the basic parameters of the project and are often the beginning points of a discussion with those involved in the project.

Scope

The scope of the Diversity Training evaluation project needs to be clearly defined. The scope can pinpoint key parameters addressed by the project. The following list shows typical scope issues that should be defined in the project:

- ▶ Target group for the evaluation

- ▶ Location of the target group

- ▶ Timeframe for the evaluation

- ▶ Technology necessary to conduct the evaluation

- ▶ Access to stakeholders

- ▶ Functional area for coverage

- ▶ Product line for coverage

- ▶ Type of Diversity Training process/activity/competencies being evaluated

- ▶ Constraints on data collection

Perhaps the project is limited to certain employee or demographic groups, a functional area of the business, a specific location, a unique type of strategy, or a precise time frame. Sometimes there is a constraint on the type of data collected or access to certain individuals, such as particular diverse customers. Whatever the scope involves, it needs to be clearly defined in this section.

Timing

Timing is critical in showing specifically when the Diversity Training activities will occur. This means not only the timing of the delivery of the final Diversity Training ROI study report but also the timing of particular steps and events — including when data are needed, analyzed, and reported and when presentations are made. The following list shows typical scheduled activities:

- ▶ Diversity Training initiatives and/or solutions developed

- ▶ Diversity Training Implementation started

- ▶ Diversity Training Implementation completed

- ▶ Start of the Diversity Training ROI evaluation project

- ▶ Data collection design completed

- ▶ Evaluation design completed

- ▶ Data collection begins

- ▶ Data collection completed

- ▶ Specific data collection issues (for example, pilot testing, executive interviews)

- ▶ Data analysis completed

- ▶ Preliminary results available

- ▶ Report developed

- ▶ Presentation to management

Deliverables from the Diversity Training Evaluation Project

This section describes exactly what your project sponsor or client will receive when the evaluation project is completed in terms of competency models, reports, documents, systems, and processes. Whatever the specific deliverables, they are clearly defined in this section. Most projects will have a final report, but they often go much further, delivering new skill sets, processes and suggested methodologies for improving the Diversity Training process or Diversity Training initiative being evaluated.

Methodology

If a specific methodology is to be used for the Diversity Training DTROI® study, it should be defined. A reference should be made to the appropriateness of the methodology, and how the methodology will accomplish what is needed for the Diversity Training evaluation project to be successful.

Steps

The specific steps that will occur should be defined showing key milestones. This provides a step-by-step understanding and tracking of the Diversity Training evaluation project such that at any given time the project sponsor or client and the diversity staff can see not only where progress is made but also where the evaluation project is going next.

Resources Required for the Diversity Training Evaluation Project

This section will define the specific resources required to implement the evaluation. This could include access to individuals, vendors, technology, equipment, facilities, competitors, or customers. All resources that may be needed should be listed along with details regarding the timing and circumstances under which the resources will be needed.

Cost

The cost section details the specific costs tied to different steps of the evaluation process. There is often reluctance to detail costs; however, it is important to understand the different steps of the process and their relative costs. When calculating the diversity return on investment for a Diversity Training initiative, all costs are considered. This includes not only development and implementation costs but also the costs of evaluating the program. We will discuss this in detail in a later chapter.

Levels of Objectives for the Diversity Training Initiative

Eventually a Diversity Training initiative or intervention should lead to some level of impact on the business of the organization. In some situations, the Diversity Training initiative is aimed at softer issues, such as improving the diverse workforce climate, employee satisfaction, diverse customer group satisfaction, and diverse workgroup conflict reduction. In other situations, Diversity Training initiatives are aimed at more tangible issues such as cost reductions, productivity, and the number of voluntary turnovers, all sorted by demographic group. Whatever the case, Diversity Training initiatives and interventions should have multiple levels of objectives. These levels of objectives, ranging from qualitative to quantitative, define precisely what will occur as a particular Diversity Training initiative is implemented in the organization. The table below highlights the different levels of objectives. These objectives are so critical that they need special attention in their development and use.

Table 3.1

Multiple Levels of Objectives for Diversity Initiatives	
Level 1: Reaction, Satisfaction , and planned actions	Defines a specific level of satisfaction and reaction to the diversity initiative as it is revealed and communicated to the stakeholders involved. Also, what actions participants plans to take as a result of the training.
Level 2: Learning	Defines specific skills and knowledge requirements as the stakeholders learn new skills and acquire new knowledge through the diversity training initiative.
Level 3: Application and Implementation	Defines key issues around the implementation of a diversity initiative in the workplace.
Level 4: Business Impact	Defines the specific business measures that will change or improve as a result of the implementation of diversity initiatives.
Level 5: Diversity Return on Investment (DROI)	Defines the specific return on investment from the implementation of the diversity initiative, comparing costs to benefits.
Level 6: Intangibles	Defines specific types of items that may surface and will be recorded as "intangibles or softer evidence" of the diversity initiative's impact.

Satisfaction, Reaction, and Planned Actions

For any Diversity Training initiative to succeed, it is important that a wide range of stakeholders respond positively to the initiative. Ideally, the stakeholders should be satisfied with the program or initiative because it offered the best possible solution to the organization's needs and that it was performed in a way that provided opportunities for "win-win" outcomes. Stakeholders are those who are directly involved in implementing or using the diversity program or intervention. This includes employees involved in implementing the diversity training initiative or the supervisors or team leaders responsible for the redesigned or changed process. Stakeholders could also be managers who must support or assist the process in some way. Finally, the stakeholders could involve the teams and task forces involved in the diversity training intervention.

It is important to routinely obtain this type of information so that feedback can be used to make some adjustments, keep the diversity initiative on track, and perhaps even redesign certain parts of a process to make it more diversity-friendly. Many diversity practitioners don't often develop specific objectives at this level nor are data collection mechanisms put in place to ensure appropriate feedback for making the needed adjustments. Participants should be given an opportunity to express their planned actions as a result of the training. This helps to provide clarity and purpose for their use of the newly acquired skills as well as begins the "Chain of Impact" link to the intervention's DTROI®.

Learning Objectives

Many diversity training programs and initiatives will involve learning objectives. Learning objectives are critical to the measurement process because they define the desired competence or performance necessary to make the diversity change program or initiative successful. Learning objectives provide a focus for those involved clearly indicating what they must learn.

The best learning objectives describe the observable and measurable behaviors that are necessary for success with the diversity initiative. They are often outcome based, clearly worded, and specific. They specify what the particular stakeholder must do as a result of implementing the diversity change initiative. Learning objectives often have three components:

1. Performance — what the participant or stakeholder will be able to do as the diversity initiative or program is implemented

2. Conditions — under which the participant or stakeholder will perform the various tasks and processes

3. Criteria — The degree or level of proficiency necessary to perform a new task, process, or procedure that is part of a diversity solution.

The three types of learning objectives are often defined as:

▶ Awareness — familiarity with terms, concepts, and processes

▶ Knowledge — general understanding of concepts, processes, or procedures

▶ Performance — ability to demonstrate skills at least on a basic level.

Application and Implementation Objectives

As a diversity solution is actually implemented in the workplace, the application and implementation objectives clearly define what is expected and often what level of performance is expected. Application objectives are similar to learning objectives but reflect the actual implementation of the new diversity initiative or program. They also involve particular milestones, indicating specifically when intervals of the process are implemented. Application objectives are critical because they describe the expected outcomes in the interim — that is, between the actual learning of new diversity tasks and procedures and the actual impact that will result. Application or implementation objectives describe how things should be performed or the state of the workplace after the diversity training initiative is implemented. They provide a basis for the evaluation of on-the-job changes and performance. The emphasis is on what has occurred on the job as a result of the diversity training initiative or change process.

The best application objectives identify behaviors that are observable and measurable or action steps in a process that can easily be observed or measured. They specify what the various stakeholders will change or have changed as a result of the diversity training initiative. As with learning objectives, application or implementation objectives may have three components:

1. Performance — describes what the stakeholders have changed or have accomplished in a specific time frame after the implementation of the diversity training initiative.

2. Conditions — specifies the circumstances under which the

stakeholders have performed or are performing the tasks or implementing the diversity training initiative.

3. Criteria — indicates the degree or level of proficiency under which the diversity training initiative is implemented, the task is being performed, or the steps are completed.

There are two types of basic application objectives. They are knowledge-based — when the general use or implementation of concepts, processes, and procedures is important — and behavior-based, which is when the diversity target group is able to demonstrate the actual use of skills, accomplishments of particular tasks, or completion of particular milestones. Here are just a few of the typical questions that are key to application and implementation objectives:

▶ What new or improved knowledge will be applied on the job?

▶ What is the frequency of the skill application?

▶ What specific new task will be performed?

▶ What new steps will be implemented?

▶ What action items will be implemented?

▶ What new procedure will be implemented or changed?

▶ What new guidelines will be implemented?

▶ What new processes will be implemented?

▶ Which meetings need to be held?

▶ Which tasks, steps, or procedures will be discontinued?

Application objectives have always been included to some degree in diversity initiatives but have not been as specific as they need to be. To be effective, they must clearly define the workplace environment when the diversity initiative is successfully implemented.

Impact Objectives

Every diversity training initiative should result in improving an organization's impact. Organizational impact represents the key business measures that should be improved as the application or implementation objectives are achieved. The impact objectives are critical to measuring business or organizational performance because they define the ultimate expected outcome from the diversity training initiative. They describe the business or organizational unit of performance that should be connected to the diversity training solution. Above all, they place emphasis on achieving bottom-line results, which stakeholders and client groups demand.

The best impact objectives contain measures that are linked to the solution from the diversity training initiative. They describe measures that are easily collected and are well known to the organization. They are results-based, are clearly worded, and specify what the stakeholders have ultimately accomplished in the organizational their unit as a result of the diversity initiative. Diversity impact objectives include items such as reduced turnover, improved diverse customer market penetration, increased ideas converted to production, improved cycle time, *etc.*

Diversity Return on Investment (DROI)

A fifth level of objectives for diversity training initiatives is the actual expected return on investment. These objectives define the expected payoff from the diversity training initiative and compare the input resources, the costs of the diversity training initiative, with the value of the ultimate outcome — the monetary benefits. This is typically expressed as a desired return on investment percentage that compares the annual monetary benefits minus the cost, divided by the actual costs, and multiplied by 100. A zero percent DROI® indicate a break-even diversity solution. A 50 percent DROI® indicates that the cost of the initiative is recaptured and an additional 50 percent "earnings" are achieved.

For many diversity interventions, the DROI® amount is often larger than what might be expected from the ROI of other expenditures, such as the purchase of a new company, a new building, or major equipment; but the two are related. In many organizations the DROI® objective is set slightly higher than the ROI expected from other interventions because of the relative newness of applying return on investment concepts to diversity training initiatives and processes. For example, if the expected ROI from the purchase of a new company is 20 percent, the DROI® from a diversity training initiative might be nearer 25-35 percent. The important point is that the DROI® objective target should be established up front through discussions with stakeholders and the client.

Importance of Specific Objectives

Developing specific objectives at different levels for a diversity training initiative is critical to the success of the effort. First, objectives provide direction to the diversity staff directly involved in the process to help keep them on track. Objectives define exactly what is expected at different time frames from different departments or individuals and involves different types of data. Also, objectives provide guidance to the support staff and key stakeholders so that they fully understand the ultimate goal and impact of the diversity training initiative. Further, objectives provide important information and motivation for the stakeholders. In most diversity training initiatives, the stakeholders are actively involved and will influence the results of the initiative. Specific objectives provide goals and motivation for the stakeholders so that they will clearly see the gains that should be achieved. More importantly, objectives provide important information for key client groups such that they can clearly understand what the outcome or environment will look like when the diversity training initiative is complete. Finally, from an evaluation perspective, the objectives provide a basis for measuring success.

Aligning and Linking Your Evaluation Strategy with Business Needs

There is a distinct linkage between evaluation objectives and original business needs driving a diversity training intervention. In this chapter, we introduced the six levels of evaluation and showed how they are critical to providing an overall assessment of the impact of a diversity training initiative. The earlier material in this chapter showed the importance of setting objectives around a diversity training initiative. The objectives define the specific improvements sought. This section highlights additional connections to the original needs assessment. The figure below shows the connection between the diversity training initiative evaluation levels and a business needs assessment.

Table 3-2

		The Hubbard Diversity Alignment / Linkage Framework			
	Levels	Business Needs Analysis	Diversity Initiative Objectives	Evaluation Type	Levels
Chain of impact	5	Potential Payoff	DROI Objectives	DROI	5
	4	Business Needs	Impact Objectives	Business Impact	4
	3	Job Performance Needs	Application and Implementation Objectives	Application and Implementation	3
	2	Skill / Knowledge / Attitude Deficiencies	Learning Objectives	Learning	2
	1	Preference for Solutions	Reaction and Satisfaction Objectives	Reaction and Satisfaction	1

Source: Adapted from J.Phillips, R. Stone, P. Phillips, "The Human Resources Scorecard," Butterworth-Heinemann, p52.

This figure shows the important linkage from the initial problem or opportunity that created the business need to the evaluation and measurement. Level 5 defines the potential payoff and examines the possibility for a diversity return on investment before the project is even pursued. Level 4 analysis focuses directly on the business needs that precipitated a diversity training initiative. At Level 3, the specific diversity issues in the workplace focus on job or interaction performance in detail. At Level 2, the specific knowledge, skill, cultural competency, or attitude deficiencies related to diversity and inclusion processes are uncovered as learning needs are identified. Finally, the preferences for the structure of the solution define the Level 1 needs. This connection is critical and important to understanding all the elements that must go into an effective diversity training intervention solution.

An example will help illustrate this linkage and alignment. The figure below shows an example of linking a business needs assessment with the diversity evaluation of a training initiative involving a reduction in absenteeism. As the figure shows, the first step is to see if the problem is great enough at level 5. However, this sometimes causes a validation of the business problem using Level 4 data. Four benchmarks are used to gauge the current absenteeism problem. These are:

▶ Absenteeism is higher than it used to be.

▶ Absenteeism is higher than at other locations within the company.

▶ Absenteeism is higher than at other facilities in the local area.

▶ Absenteeism is higher than the general manager desires.

With the confirmation in Level 4 that there is a problem, a potential payoff is estimated. This involves estimating the cost of absenteeism and estimating the actual potential reduction that can come from the diversity intervention. This develops a profile of potential payoff to see if the problem is worth solving.

At Level 3, the causes of excessive absenteeism are explored using a variety of techniques. One issue that is uncovered is that a "business-based flexibility" work life policy covering flextime arrangements is not currently being applied in an equitable way to all employees by managers. A pareto analysis revealed that the primary reported reasons for unexpected absences were due to daycare and elder-care responsibilities and the lack of manager flexibility in each business unit to adjust to employee family requirements. A learning component at Level 2 is also uncovered because the team leaders need to understand how and when to administer the business-based flexibility policies. It was discovered that manager cultural and other biases determined who would be allowed to utilize the policy and for what purpose. Finally, the specific way in which the diversity training initiative should be implemented is explored in terms of preferences at Level 1. In this case, supervisors preferred to attend a half-day meeting to learn how the policies should be implemented and leave with a job aid that helps them with the process as they apply it.

Table 3-3

Levels	Business Needs Analysis	Diversity Initiative Objectives	Evaluation Type	Levels
5	Problem is causing serious costs	DROI of 25%	Calculate the DROI	5
4	An Absenteeism problem exists when compared with four benchmarks	Weekly absenteeism rate will reduce	Monitor absenteeism data for 6 months	4
3	Flexible work hours process is not currently applied equitably by managers	Business-based Flexibility policy used correctly in 95% of situations to address employee family care needs that result in absences	Follow-up questionnaire to managers and employees in 3 months (frequency of use)	3
2	Need to understand how to administer the new business-based flexibility policy	Learn how and when to use the Business-based Flexibility policy	Self-assessment checklist on key items	2
1	Managers prefer to attend a half-day meeting and have a job-aid	New Business-based flexibility policy training receives a rating of 4 out of 5	Reaction questionnaire at the end of the meeting	1

These five levels provide an overall profile for determining if the problem is worth solving to begin with, as well as aligning problems with key measures and data necessary to develop the diversity training initiative's objectives. The diversity training initiatives objectives for each level are shown in the figure as well, as are the evaluation methods needed to verify that the appropriate changes did occur. This process is important to the development and implementation of a diversity business solution. Many diversity stakeholders are involved in developing the actual solution and implementing the solution, as is the case in this particular example. When this occurs, the above linkage connects the needs to actual business objectives and then to the training evaluation process.

The solution to the problem or opportunity is an important part of this linkage and alignment. Some diversity professionals may be involved in uncovering needs with the initial analysis to determine the actual causes of the problem and then recommend solutions. It is up to the client or business unit to then implement the solution, or implementation becomes part of another diversity initiative. In both cases, the solutions are ultimately developed. If this has not been accomplished, multiple levels of analysis may be necessary for the intervention. Although other resources and references exist that focus more specifically on the performance analysis to uncover different levels of needs, a brief summary is presented here.

Payoff Needs

The very first part of the process is to determine if the problem is worth solving or if the opportunity is large enough to warrant serious consideration. In some cases, this is obvious when serious problems are affecting the organization's operations and strategy.

Still others may not be so obvious. At Level 5, it is important not only to identify needed business improvement measures but to convert them into monetary values so the actual improvement can be converted to financial measures.

The second part of the process is to develop an approximate cost for the entire diversity initiative. This could come from a detailed proposal or may be a rough estimate. At this stage it is only an estimate because the projected cost of the project is compared to the potential benefits to roughly determine if a payoff would result from addressing the issue. This step may be omitted in some situations when the problem must be solved regardless of the cost or if it becomes obvious that it is a high-payoff activity. Still other projects may be initiated when the potential payoff is not expected to be developed. For example, as an organization strives to be a technology leader, it may be difficult to place a value on that goal.

Business Needs

In conjunction with Level 5, actual business data are examined to determine which measures need to improve. This includes an examination of organizational records and involves examining all types of hard and soft data. Usually one of the data items and its performance trigger the diversity training initiative or intervention-for example, market share may not be as much as it should be, costs may be excessive, quality may be deteriorating, or productivity may not be as high as it should be. These are the key issues that come directly from the data in the organization and are often found in the operating reports or records. They may indicate the need for diversity and inclusion-based training or other interventions.

The supporting data may come not only from the operating reports but from annual reports, employee opinion data, engagement surveys, multicultural marketing data, and industry data, major planning documents or other important information sources that clearly indicate challenges in the organization's operating performance in terms of its operation or its strategy or both.

Job Performance Needs

The Level 3 analysis involves job performance or workplace needs. The task is to determine the cause of the problem as determined at Level 4 (that is, what is causing the business measure not to be at the desired level or to be inhibited in some way). These needs can vary considerably and may include, among others, dealing with the following:

- ▶ Ineffective or inappropriate behavior

- ▶ Prejudice and stereotypes

- ▶ Dysfunctional work climate

- ▶ Ineffective systems

- ▶ Institutionalized bias in management practices

- ▶ Improper process flow due to cross-functional team issues

- ▶ Ethnocentrism

- ▶ Ineffective procedures

- ► Inter-group conflict

- ► Unsupported culture

- ► Inappropriate technology

- ► Unsupportive environment

These and other types of workplace needs will have to be uncovered using a variety of problem-solving or analysis techniques. This may involve the use of data collection techniques such as surveys, questionnaires, focus groups, or interviews. It may involve a variety of six sigma-based problem-solving or analysis techniques such as root-cause analysis, fishbone diagrams, and other analysis techniques. Whatever is used, the key is to determine all the causes of the problem so that solutions can be developed. Often, multiple solutions are appropriate.

Learning Needs

Most problem analysis from Level 3 uncovers specific learning needs. It may be that learning inefficiencies, in terms of knowledge and skills, may contribute to the problem if they are not the major cause of it. In other situations, the actual solution applied may need a particular learning component as participants learn how to implement a new process, procedure, or system in a multicultural global environment. The extent of learning required will determine whether formalized diversity and inclusion training is needed or if more informal, on-the-job methods can be used to build the necessary cultural competency, skills and knowledge.

The learning would typically involve acquisition of knowledge or the development of diversity-related skills necessary to improve the situation. In some cases, perceptions or attitudes may need to be altered to make the situation more successful in the future.

Preferences

The final level is to consider the preference for the solution. This involves determining the way in which those involved in the process prefer to have it changed or implemented. It may involve implementation preferences and/or learning preferences. Learning preferences may involve decisions such as when learning is expected and in what amounts, how it is presented, and the overall time frame. Implementation preferences may involve issues such as timing, support, expectation, and other key factors. The important point is to try to determine the specific preferences to the extent possible so that the complete profile of the solution can be adjusted accordingly.

Once all avenues of the planning process are addressed, it is time to begin your data collection effort.

Collecting Data During a Diversity Training Initiative

Introduction

Data collection is the most crucial step of the evaluation process because without data, there is no evidence of the diversity training initiative's impact and therefore no need for an evaluation. During the data collection process, it is necessary to determine the participant's reactions and satisfaction to the diversity initiative (Level 1), their level of learning from the intervention (Level 2), the amount of application and implementation that happened as a consequence of the diversity training initiative (Level 3), the resulting business impact (Level 4), and whether the initiative generated benefits and a return on investment (Levels 5 and 6). It is necessary to collect data from at least levels 1-4 because of the "Chain of Impact" that must exist for a diversity initiative to be successful. To reap the chain of impact: a Key business problem that can be addressed by diversity and inclusion must be identified, participants in the diversity training initiative related to this business problem should experience a positive reaction to the initiative and its potential applications and they should acquire new knowledge or skills to perform at an improved level as a result of the training initiative. As application and/or implementation opportunities arise, there should be changes in their "on-the-job" behavior that result in a positive impact on the organization. The only way to know if the chain of impact has occurred up to this point is to collect data at all four levels. The diversity training initiative will also generate benefits that are either quantitative or qualitative in the forms of "benefit-to-cost" impacts, dollar return-on-investment based, and/or anecdotal. If this is the case, all six levels of evaluation will be involved as shown:

Table 3-4

Level of Data Analysis	Type of Data
1	Reaction / Satisfaction and planned action(s)
2	Learning
3	Application / implementation
4	Business impact
5	Diversity Return on Investment (DROI^{tm})
6	Anecdotal

Measuring Reaction and Satisfaction

Collecting reaction and satisfaction data during the implementation of a diversity training initiative is the first operational phase of the DROI process. Participant feedback data are powerful for making adjustments and measuring success. A variety of methods are available to capture reaction and satisfaction data at appropriate times during the implementation process. We will examine some of the more common approaches for collecting these data and highlight several key issues about the use of the information.

Why Measure Reaction and Satisfaction?

It would be difficult to imagine a diversity training initiative being implemented without collecting feedback from those involved in the process, or at least from the client. Client feedback is critical to understand how well the process is working or to gauge its success after it has been completed. It is always included in every diversity training initiative because of its crucial importance. However, the advantage of collecting this type of data goes beyond just the satisfaction of the client and includes many other key issues, making it one of the most important data collection efforts. The advantages may include:

- ▶ Measuring Diverse Customer Service Impact

- ▶ Determining if the Initiative is On-Target

- ▶ Making Adjustment and Changes

- ▶ Collecting Participant Reactions and Planned Actions

- ▶ Expected Involvement

- ▶ Comparing with Data from Other Programs

Measuring Diverse Customer Service Impact

Multicultural Customer service approaches are a critical element for organizational success in today's economy, therefore it is important to measure reactions across demographic groups. Both internal organizational customers and diverse customers in new emerging ethnic markets have a variety of needs that must be fulfilled. Without continuous improvement feedback evidenced by customer satisfaction data, you will not know if your internal or external diversity initiatives and interventions are successful. It is also important to consider the different types of customers that may be involved in your initiative. First, there are those directly involved in the training initiative. They are the key stakeholders who are directly affected by the diversity training initiative and often have to change their behavior, processes, or procedures and make other adjustments related to the initiative. In addition, they often have to learn new skills, tasks, and behaviors to make the training initiative successful. These participants are critical to the success of the initiative and their feedback is vital to making adjustments and changes in the training initiative or interventions as it unfolds and is implemented. For example, a training program related to the new advertising campaign to attract minorities might have a reaction focused feedback tool to use during an on-campus focus group session, or during a test market product release, or in a specific locale to determine diverse consumer reaction to a Service Rep's delivery (using cultural intelligence information) of the new advertisement or product service strategy. The organization would use this feedback to adjust the Service Rep's training to meet its target objectives.

The second set of customers is those who support from the sidelines; those who are not directly involved, but have some interest in the diversity training initiative. For example, this group might include specific storeowners who will carry the new product or service shown in the advertisement for these ethnic consumers. Their perception of the success of the diversity training initiative or its potential success is important feedback. And, as a group, they are always in a strong position to influence the outcome of the campaign.

The third set of stakeholders is perhaps the most important group, since they include individuals such as the client or financial sponsor who pays for the diversity training initiative or influences its budget approval, allocates resources, and ultimately lives with the success or failure of the diversity training initiative. This important group must be completely satisfied with the diversity training initiative as a solution. Their level of satisfaction must be determined early, and adjustments must be made. In short, customer satisfaction is key to success and must be obtained in a variety of different ways to focus on the success.

Determining if the Initiative is On-Target

Diversity training initiatives can go off in the wrong direction, sometimes very quickly. You may discover that the particular diversity training initiative is the wrong or incomplete solution for the business challenge it was designed to address. There are times when the diversity training initiative will be mismatched from the beginning, so it is essential to obtain feedback early in the process such that adjustments can be made. This helps avoid misunderstandings, miscommunications, and more importantly, misappropriations, before more serious problems are created.

Making Adjustment and Changes

It is critical to obtain feedback throughout the duration of a diversity training initiative to make refinements and adjustments. There must be an important linkage between obtaining feedback and making changes and reporting changes back to the groups who provide the information. Customers, for example, will want to know if you used the feedback that they supplied to improve the diversity training intervention. This survey-feedback-action loop is vital to the success of any diversity initiative.

Collecting Participant Reactions

Many of the individuals involved in the diversity training initiative, particularly the affected populations or participants appreciate the opportunity to provide feedback. In too many situations, their input is ignored and their complaints disregarded. This happens often when assumptions are made that this population is just like all others. For example, some advertisers will assume just because an advertisement worked well for the Caucasian majority market that all that is needed to sell to minorities is to replace the images with a minority. What they may forget is that the culture, background, specific situation and other aspects of the advertisement do not match what a person from that culture would do or how they would respond. Employee Resource or Affinity Groups can be a great source of information and feedback for diversity training initiative development and implementation if they are utilized properly. These groups appreciate it when they are asked for input and, more importantly when action is taken as a result of their input. Other stakeholders and even clients appreciate the opportunity to provide feedback, not only early in the process, but throughout the process.

Expected Involvement

For some, collecting this type of feedback data is expected as the norm. In fact, if you did not collect it, your training evaluation process will be suspect. Every diversity training initiative should have some form of reaction and satisfaction level data collection that takes place. Unfortunately, some diversity practitioners stop here and only use reaction and satisfaction level data to measure the success of the diversity training intervention. As this book will certainly illustrate, reaction and satisfaction level feedback is only one part of the evaluation puzzle and represents only one of the six types of data that can be collected. Nonetheless, its importance in the diversity training evaluation process cannot be underestimated.

Comparing with Data from Other Programs

Some organizations collect reaction and satisfaction data from several sources using standard questions, and the data are then compared with data from other diversity training initiatives so that norms and standards can be developed. This is particularly helpful at the end of a diversity training initiative rollout when client satisfaction is assessed. These satisfaction data can be used not only to compare the success of the initiative but to relate to the overall success of the initiative and even correlate with other successful measures. Data collection must be deliberately pursued in a systematic, logical and rational way.

Areas of Feedback for Reaction and Satisfaction Data

There are many topics that are critical targets for feedback because there are so many issues and processes involved in a typical diversity training initiative implementation. Feedback is needed in almost every major issue, step, or process to make sure things are moving forward properly. The following list shows the typical major areas of reaction and satisfaction feedback for many initiatives:

- ▶ Appropriateness of objectives

- ▶ Appropriateness of plans

- ▶ Appropriateness of schedule

- ▶ Progress made with plans

- ▶ Relevance of initiative

- ▶ Support for initiative

- ▶ Resources for initiative

- ▶ Integration of initiative with other systems

- ▶ Initiative leadership

- ▶ Initiative staffing

- ▶ Initiative coordination

- ▶ Initiative communication

- ► Motivation of initiative participants

- ► Cooperation of initiative participants

- ► Capability of initiative participants

- ► Likelihood of initiative success

- ► Barriers to project success

- ► Enablers to initiative success

- ► Continuing administration of the initiative

This list shows the key success factors in a diversity training initiative, beginning with the issues that reflect the initial planning of the initiative. Different stakeholders react to the appropriateness of the training initiative planning schedule and objectives and the progress made with those planning tools. The relevance of the initiative is critical for the participants because if the initiative is perceived as irrelevant, more than likely it will not succeed in the workplace. The support for the initiative—including resources and how the initiative is integrated with other systems—represent important areas for feedback. Participants must see the initiative has the necessary commitment. Several issues are important to management and the organization sponsoring the initiative, including initiative leadership, staffing levels, coordination, and communication. Also, it is important to gather feedback on how well the initiative implementation team is working to address such issues as motivation, cooperation, and capability. A dysfunctional team can spell disaster quickly. Finally, the issues that inhibit or enhance success are important, along with input on the likelihood of success. For a particular initiative, there can be other issues, and each can have specific parts. Each step, element, task, or part of the diversity training initiative represents an opportunity for feedback. The challenge is to sort out those things that are most important so the participants can provide valuable input.

Measuring Skill and Knowledge Changes

It may seem unnecessary to measure learning in a diversity training initiative. After all, when application and implementation are measured, the actual progress made in the workplace is measured. And ultimately, when business impact variable are monitored, the success of the initiative becomes quite clear. However, it is sometimes critical to understand the extent to which learning has occurred, particularly in initiatives where there are a significant amount of team changes, procedure changes, new tools, new processes, and new technologies. The extent to which participants in the diversity training initiative learn their role behavior, the new procedure change or new process, can often make or break the success of the diversity training initiative.

There are three key areas that determine why it is important to measure learning in a diversity training initiative. Each of them on their own would be enough to justify why learning is measured. Taken together, they represent a powerful thrust and present strategic evidence for the amount of skill, knowledge, or change that occurred during the diversity initiative.

Measuring Knowledge, Expertise, and Competencies is Important

Working in today's world requires the use of a wide range of competencies, skills and behaviors. Having and/or acquiring core competencies and capabilities in a variety of technical, process, cultural, and interpersonal areas is a chief determinate of success in a multicultural world. Many diversity training initiatives will test the use and application of this knowledge, expertise and competency. Therefore, measuring whether participants in a diversity training initiative actually acquired the intellectual knowledge base to function effectively in a diverse work environment is crucial.

Diversity training initiatives often require employees to learn new approaches, develop expertise in processes and cultural systems that are different from what they are used to. Many of these diversity interventions ask that they increase their competence in cultural awareness and cross-cultural interaction skills in areas where this new learning runs counter to their current cultural/behavioral software programming. Learning represents a large part of a diversity training initiative since many employees do not automatically use effective skills when interacting with others who are different and with systems that operate using new cultural norms. Gone are the homogeneous organizational environments where the employee mixtures are generally flat and the complexion somewhat predictable at each level. Instead, there are complex, diverse environments, complex human and other processes, and tools that must be used in intelligent ways to reap the benefits of a diverse workforce and society. Employees must learn in a variety of ways to gain the skills and competencies necessary to utilize the rich diversity reflected in all aspects of their environment and what they do. Also, diverse work team leaders and managers often serve to reinforce, coach, and mentor employees in their use of newly learned skills to ensure that learning is transferred to the job and the diversity initiative is implemented as planned.

Finding Out What Went Wrong When There is a Problem

If you want to find out what went wrong during the rollout of a diversity training initiative, and/or what needs to be changed, it is critical to measure and evaluate learning. It is helpful to learn:

- ▶ What went wrong?

- ▶ What areas need adjustment?

- ▶ What needs to be altered completely?

- ▶ What portion of the initiative that required learning was learned?

- ▶ What portion of the initiative that required learning was not learned?

When learning is measured, it is easy to track down whether learning was the problem or something else. Without the learning component, diversity professionals will not know why employees are not performing the way they should or which part of the diversity training initiative is not being managed properly. These critical issues make learning an important consideration in a diversity measurement strategy. Competency and skill-based learning helps build strategic diversity capability that can be used as a competitive advantage.

Collecting Data After a Diversity Training Initiative

Measuring Application and Implementation

Measuring the actual application and implementation of skills and knowledge is critical because these steps play a pivotal role in the overall success or failure of a diversity training initiative. If it is learned that skills and knowledge are not applied effectively, there will be no change in the business function-and no benefit from the diversity training initiative.

Why Measure Application and Implementation?

In addition to the obvious reasons for measuring application and implementation, there are several specific reasons why this is one of the most important measures to track in the diversity evaluation process.

The Value of the Information. The value of the information increases as progress is made through the chain of impact from Level 1 to Level 5. Thus, information concerning application and implementation at Level 3 is more valuable to the client or business unit than reaction/satisfaction (Level 1) and learning

(Level 2). This is not meant to discount the importance of these two levels, but to emphasize that measuring the extent to which the diversity initiative is implemented often provides critical data about not only the success of the project but also the factors that can contribute to greater success as the diversity initiative is fully integrated within the organization.

A Key Transition Issue. The two previous measures, reaction / satisfaction and learning, occur during the diversity training initiative where there is more attention and focus directly on the diversity training initiative. Level 3, measuring application and implementation, occur after the diversity intervention has been implemented and measures the success of the application and implementation. Essentially, this measure explains the degree to which the diversity training initiative is handed off to those who are charged with its ultimate success. This is a key transition process and is the first measure that follows the process after the diversity training initiative has been fully implemented. This in itself makes it a critical issue, where various measures of success are identified and enhancements to additional success are pinpointed.

The Key Focus of Many Diversity Interventions. As many diversity interventions focus directly on application and implementation, the diversity initiative's sponsor often speaks in these terms and is concerned about these measures of success. Many major diversity training interventions designed to transform an organization and build a stronger team and customer focus will have key issues around Level 3, application and implementation. The sponsor will be interested in knowing the extent to which all of the key stakeholders are adjusting to and implementing the desired new (inclusive) behaviors, processes, and procedures. This interest is at the core of application and implementation.

Problems, Obstacles, and Barriers. When a diversity training initiative goes astray, the first question is, "What happened?" More importantly, when an initiative appears not to be adding value, the first question should be, "What can we do to change the direction of the intervention?" In either scenario, it is critical to have information that identifies barriers to success, problems encountered in implementation, and obstacles to the actual application of the process or skill. It is at Level 3, measuring application and implementation, that these problems are addressed, identified, and examined for solutions. In many cases, the key stakeholders directly involved in the process provide important input into the recommendations for making changes or for using a different approach in the future.

Enablers and Enhancers. When there is success, the obvious question is, "How can we repeat this or even improve on this in the future?" The answer to this question is also found at Level 3. Identifying the factors that contribute directly to the success of the diversity initiative is critical because those same items can be used to replicate the process to produce specific results in the future and to enhance results. When key stakeholders identify those issues, it helps make the project successful and provides an important case history of what is necessary for success.

Rewards Those Who Are Most Effective. Measuring application and implementation allows the client, the business unit, and the Diversity staff to reward those who are doing the best job of applying the processes and implementing the diversity training initiative. Measures taken at this level provide clear evidence of various efforts and roles, providing an excellent basis for performance review or special recognition. This often has a reinforcing value for keeping the project on track and communicating a strong message for future improvements.

Measuring Business Impact

Measuring and tracking business performance measures helps to bring the diversity training evaluation process full circle to connect with the initial business needs analysis. Some diversity staff members-and clients-regard business impact data as the most important type because of their connection to business unit success. Also, less-than-desired results in business measures are what translate into a business need that ultimately initiate the diversity training intervention.

Why Measure Business Impact?

Although there are several obvious reasons for measuring impact, four particular issues support the rationale for collecting business impact data related to a diversity initiative.

Higher-level Data. Following the assumption that higher-level data create more value for the client, the business impact measures in a five-level framework offer more valuable data. They are the data considered to be the consequence of the application and implementation of a diversity training initiative. They often represent the bottom-line measures that are positively influenced when a program is successful.

A Business Driver for Diversity Initiatives. For most diversity training initiatives, the business impact data represent the initial drivers for the diversity initiative. It is the problem of deterioration or less-than-desired performance, or the opportunity for improvement of a business measure that often leads to a diversity initiative. If the business needs defined by business measures are the drivers for a project, then the key measure for evaluating the project is the business impact. The extent to which measures actually have changed is the key determinant of the success of the project.

Payoff with Clients. Business impact data often reflect key payoff measures from the perspective of the client (internal and/or external). These are the measures often desired by the client and that the client wants to see changed or improved. They often represent hard, indisputable facts that reflect performance critical to the business and operating unit level of the organization.

Easy to Measure. One unique feature about business impact data is that they are often very easy to measure. Hard and soft data measures at this level often reflect key measures that are found in plentiful numbers throughout an organization. It is not unusual for an organization to have hundreds or even thousands of measures reflecting specific business impact items. The challenge is to connect the diversity training initiative objectives to the appropriate business measures. This is more easily accomplished at the beginning of the diversity training initiative due to the availability and ease with which many of the data items can be located.

Reviewing Historical Data

Another alternative for identifying diversity measurement areas is reviewing historical data. Data are available in every organization to measure performance. Monitoring performance data enables you to measure diversity results in terms of output, quality, costs, and time. In determining the use of data in the diversity training intervention, the first consideration should include examining databases and reports. In most organizations, performance data suitable for measuring improvements from a diversity training initiative are available. If not, additional record-keeping systems will have to be developed for data collection, measurement, and analysis.

At this point, as with many other points in the process, the question of economics enters. Is it economical to develop the record-keeping system necessary to evaluate a diversity training initiative? If the costs are greater than the expected return for the entire program, then it is meaningless to develop them.

Using Current Measures

When using current measures, be sure they are appropriate to the area you want to study. Performance measures should be thoroughly researched to identify those that are related to the proposed objectives of the diversity training initiative. Frequently, an organization will have several performance measures related to the same item. For example, if the diversity organization works with the operations department to improve the efficiency of a production unit's work team, it might start by analyzing diverse work team creativity and innovation processes and the degree of inclusion of a demographic group in the process. The output/ outcome side of this impact of this could be measured in a variety of ways:

▶ The number of units produced per hour

▶ The number of on-schedule production units

▶ The percent of utilization of the new work style

▶ The percentage of work group downtime due to conflict

▶ The labor cost per unit of production

▶ The overtime required per piece of production, and

▶ The total unit cost

Each of these, in its own way, measures the efficiency of the production unit. All related measures should be reviewed to determine those most relevant to the diversity training initiative.

Convert Current Measures to Usable Ones

Occasionally, existing performance measures are integrated with other data, and it may be difficult to keep them isolated from unrelated data. In this situation, all existing related measures should be extracted and re-tabulated to be more appropriate for comparison in the evaluation.

At times, conversion factors may be necessary. For example, the average number of new recruits per month may be presented regularly in the performance measures for the staffing department. In addition, the cost of generating new recruits per recruiter (based upon a new training program to improve recruiter use of diverse talent pipelines) is also presented. However in the evaluation of the impact of a diversity initiative, the "average cost of a diverse hire" is needed. This will require at least two existing performance records to develop the data necessary for comparison (the average number and the cost data).

Develop A Data Collection Plan for Performance Data

A data collection plan defines when, by whom, and where the data are collected. This plan should contain provisions for the evaluator to secure copies of performance reports in a timely manner so that the items can be recorded and are available for analysis.

Developing New Measures

In some cases, data are not available for the information needed to measure the effectiveness of a diversity training initiative's impact. The Diversity organization must work with the appropriate department to develop record-keeping systems, if this is economically feasible. In one organization, a new employee orientation program was implemented on a company-wide basis for new hires from diverse backgrounds. Several feedback measures were planned, including early turnover (known as survival and loss rates) — representing the percentage of people of color who left the company in the first six months of their employment. At the time of the initiative's inception, this measure was not available. When the initiative was implemented, the organization had to begin collecting early turnover figures for comparison.

Table 3-5

Typical Questions When Creating New Measures
Which department will develop the measurement system?
Who will record and monitor the data?
Where will the information be recorded?
How often will you collect data?

These questions will usually involve other departments or a management decision that extends beyond the scope of the diversity organization. Possibly the administration division, the HR Department, or Information Technology Department will be instrumental in helping determine if new measures are needed and if so, how they will be collected.

An effective diversity training initiative must be built on a comprehensive planning and data collection model that incorporates appropriate evaluation objectives and critical factual information. By utilizing these techniques to plan and collect data, your diversity training evaluation study will begin on a solid foundation that positions your diversity training initiative for success.

References:

Hubbard, Edward E., *How to Calculate Diversity Return on Investment*, Global Insights Publishing, Petaluma, CA, 1999

Phillips, Jack J., Stone, Ron D., & Pulliam Phillips, Patricia, *The Human Resources Scorecard*, Butterworth-Heinemann, 2001.

CHAPTER 4

Conducting a Diversity Training Needs and Requirements Analysis

Introduction

Measuring the ROI of Diversity Training initiatives requires Diversity Professionals and Practitioners understand and utilize the full range of measurement sciences and approaches the Training field has to offer. If our work is to be seen as credible and providing value to the organization, we must hold ourselves to a high standard whether or not the C-suite and others are asking for it. It is disheartening to know that although Donald Kirkpatrick's "Four Levels" of training measurement has been around since the 1950's, and a primary intervention in the Diversity and Inclusion field is diversity training, only a select few Diversity Professionals and Practitioners consistently use a comprehensive, Instructional Systems Design (ISD) research-based approach to diversity training evaluation.

It is regrettable, yet understandable, that Diversity Training is attacked as "having little or no value for the money invested." Many of the diversity measurement processes used by some practitioners can barely pass a true Level 1: Reaction, Satisfaction, and Planned Actions evaluation instrument test. A majority of the instrumentation found qualifies only as a basic "smile" sheet at best. This doesn't mean that credible, research-based Diversity training evaluation and initiatives do not take place in our industry, only that many Practitioners have not consistently utilized solid, DROI®-based measurement sciences to document their impact on the organization.

Using the methods and approaches described in this book, you can help change this view of Diversity Training and our field. It will give you the skills you need to begin developing a comprehensive Diversity Training measurement and evaluation system.

What is Diversity Training Evaluation?

Diversity Training evaluation is a feedback tool that promotes continuous quality improvements for Diversity training programs. Diversity Training evaluation provides the information you need to continuously improve all stages of the ISD process (Fisher, Ruffino, 1996). Often, individuals view Diversity training evaluation as a one time, final step in the Diversity training process. It is critical that evaluation is conducted as an iterative, ongoing process.

Why Evaluate Diversity Training?

Diversity Training evaluations can help the organization reach many different goals during the life cycle of a Diversity training program. One primary reason to conduct a Diversity Training evaluation is to determine if the benefits derived from the Diversity training program justified the costs. Here are some additional reasons to conduct a Diversity Training evaluation:

▶ To determine how well the Diversity training initiative met the participants' needs.

▶ To determine to what extent the participants mastered the Diversity training content.

▶ To identify whether the Diversity training methods and media helped participants achieve the learning objectives.

▶ To assess how much of the Diversity training content, including newly acquired knowledge and skills, transferred to on-the-job behaviors.

▶ To determine whether the results of the Diversity training contributed to the achievement of organization's goals. (Fisher, Ruffino, 1996)

▶ To determine the Diversity Return on Investment (DROI®) achieved by the initiative.

When Diversity training evaluations are not conducted, the following consequences may result:

- ▶ Participants may continue to take Diversity courses in which they fail to learn.

- ▶ Diversity course modifications may not be based on participant outcome data, and changes may cause effective training activities to be replaced by ineffective activities.

- ▶ Diversity Training may be viewed as a wasteful use of resources.

- ▶ Diversity Training initiatives lose credibility and brand respect with stakeholders.

- ▶ The organization's business results never reap the benefits of an effective Diversity strategy deployment and solution.

This chapter reviews information about diversity training evaluation and its relationship within the Instructional Systems Design (ISD) process. It is important to understand that diversity training evaluation is one of five phases of ISD and not an isolated function.

The ISD Process

ISD is a systems approach to analyzing, designing, developing, implementing, and evaluating any type of training. Each phase of the ISD process provides information that feeds directly into the next phase. Each phase must be completed before moving on to the next phase. If a phase is skipped, the process being used is not ISD.

Professionally created diversity training follows this five phased process: Analysis, Design, Development, Implementation, and Evaluation. This model is commonly referred to as the "ADDIE model," after the first letter of each word. In the ADDIE model, **analysis** is the input for the instructional system; **design**, **development**, and **evaluation** are the process; and **implementation** is the output. These elements overlap somewhat, depending on the project, and because the instructional system is dynamic, there will be some sharing of duties.

Phase 1: Analysis

The analytical phase is sometimes referred to as a "front-end analysis," "needs assessment," or "needs analysis." An effective needs analysis answers the following questions:

▶ What is the problem?

▶ Is Diversity training the answer to the problem?

▶ What knowledge and skills should be included in the Diversity training course?

▶ Who needs to be trained?

Analysis is the data-gathering element of Diversity training design. Here Diversity Instructional Designers assemble all the information they can possibly gather about the strategic business problem or opportunity before they consider anything else. Decisions about every aspect of the project must eventually be made. The information that Diversity Instructional Designers gather at this stage will be put to use throughout the Diversity Training initiative process, so it is necessary that they have every scrap of data to ensure the training design will be successful.

Phase 2: Design

After the problems have been defined and trainees and course outcomes have been determined, it is time to begin the design phase. During this phase, a training "blueprint" is developed that includes:

- ▶ Learning objectives

- ▶ Content outlines

- ▶ Course structure

- ▶ Training methods and media

Design is the blueprinting stage of instructional systems during which Diversity instructional designers create the blueprint for a project with all the specifications necessary to complete the project. During this stage, Diversity instructional designers write the objectives, construct course content, and complete the design plan.

Phase 3: Development

The next phase of the ISD process is the development of the Diversity training course. The steps in this phase are:

Step 1: Develop a draft set of training materials.

Step 2: Pilot test the training materials with the target audience and make the necessary revisions.

Step 3: Finalize the training materials.

Materials production and pilot testing are the hallmarks of development. Everything from lecture notes to virtual reality is brought from design to deliverable. Before Diversity instructional designers move from development to implementation, it is wise for them to do pilot testing to ensure that deliverables do not have to be redeveloped. Because of the time and expense involved, no one wants to reprint manuals or recode a technology-based project after a project goes into implementation. The pilot testing process allows organizations to implement any necessary changes in the project before the expenses associated with materials development are realized. The time and effort expended in pilot testing is well worth the effort, if for this reason alone. Pilot testing also helps designers feel confident that what they have designed works.

Phase 4: Implementation

The most familiar of the elements is implementation. The implementation phase involves conducting the Diversity training program and completing any related follow-up activities to ensure the transfer of learning to the job setting. At implementation, the design plan meets the leaner, and the content is delivered. The evaluation process that most Diversity designers and learners are familiar with takes place in this element. Diversity Training evaluation is used to gauge the degree to which learners meet objectives and facilitators or technologies deliver the expected outcomes.

Phase 5: Evaluation

The final phase of the ISD process is to determine whether the Diversity training was successful. Because Diversity Training evaluation is the focus of this book, the following questions will be answered next:

- ▶ What is Diversity training evaluation?

- ▶ Why evaluate Diversity training?

- ▶ What are Diversity training evaluation levels?

- ▶ How is the Diversity training analysis and Diversity evaluation linked?

- ▶ How is an effective Diversity training evaluation conducted?

Evaluation doesn't deserve to be listed last in the ADDIE model because it takes place in every element and surrounds the Diversity instructional design process. Evaluation is a constant guard at the gate of failure. The advantages of using an instructional system are numerous, the most important being the ability to design Diversity projects quickly and efficiently. Nothing is left to chance or ignored when a Diversity instructional designer stays within the framework of the ADDIE or other ISD models. One possible disadvantage is the necessity of a designer to be familiar with the ISD process. It is my contention that an effective ROI-based Diversity Training evaluation initiative cannot be completed unless the Diversity Training initiative's design was built using the ADDIE methodology and a behaviorally specific competency model built on correctly structured objectives.

Importance of Needs Analysis

Needs analysis is the cornerstone of training. It provides you with appropriate justification for either developing or not developing diversity instruction. You must conduct a needs analysis, no matter how abbreviated, before any instructional development takes place.

The objectives of needs analysis are to:

▶ Describe the exact nature of a performance discrepancy

▶ Determine the cause(s) of the discrepancy

▶ Recommend the appropriate solution(s)

▶ Describe the learner population

In general, Needs Analysis consists of the following steps, which do not necessarily have to be performed in the sequence given.

▶ Step 1: Identify and describe the performance discrepancies.

▶ Step 2: Determine the causes of the discrepancies.

▶ Step 3: Identify those performance discrepancies that are based on lack of skill or knowledge. Then identify the skills and knowledge needed that is related to diversity and diversity competence.

▶ Step 4: Determine whether diversity training is a viable solution.

▶ Step 5: Recommend solutions.

▶ Step 6: Describe the performer's role in behaviorally specific terms and the roles related to diversity excellence and performance.

How Are Diversity Training Analysis and Evaluation Linked?

A needs analysis establishes the criteria for measuring the success of training after its completion. A thorough needs analysis should answer the question:

"What good *will* training do?"

A thorough Diversity ROI training evaluation will answer the question:

"What good *did* training do and what was the Return on Investment (DTROI®)?"

An effective Diversity ROI training evaluation **cannot** be conducted unless a needs analysis has been completed. You cannot determine what was accomplished by a Diversity training program unless you have first defined what the program was intended to accomplish. The Diversity training needs analysis provides you with baseline measures against which to judge your Diversity training efforts.

Assessment and the Training Needs Analysis

Another link exists between training evaluation and training needs analysis. Your Diversity training evaluation can provide you with an assessment of how well you identified the training needs. If your training evaluation finds a lack of skill transfer between the training setting and the work environment, then you may have missed something in your original training needs analysis. When Diversity training success in the classroom does not translate to new on-the-job behaviors, then the needs analysis may have:

- ▶ Made inaccurate assumptions about how the training participants will use what is taught in the classroom when they return to the work environment.

- ▶ Identified different standards for use in the training from those required in the work environment.

- ▶ Failed to uncover non-training barriers (*e.g.*, reinforcements, resources, supervision) to task performance.

An effective training needs analysis avoids the common pitfalls by supplying information and increasing the likelihood that skills learned in Diversity training will transfer to the work environment.

The Primary Focus of a Diversity Needs Analysis

In needs analysis, you focus on the total performance environment and not solely on diversity. In addition you must focus on the specific job or function associated with the performance discrepancy. In needs analysis, you do not assume that diversity training will be the appropriate intervention to address the performance discrepancy.

The total performance environment includes several factors that affect performance, such as:

▶ The physical environment

▶ The feedback system

▶ Motivational/incentive factors

▶ Job/organization design

▶ Level of skill and knowledge among employees

Each of these factors may create or contribute to the performance discrepancy. Your objective is to determine the reasons underlying the discrepancy. Of the five factors listed above, only performance discrepancies resulting from a lack of skill or knowledge (such as a lack of skill in resolving interpersonal conflicts with others who are different from yourself) point to training as a solution. It has been estimated that only 20 percent of all training requests actually stem from a need for training. The remaining 80 percent of the requests stem from the other underlying causes. This fact provides a good reason for conducting a needs analysis first and not rushing ahead to develop a Diversity training program.

Analyzing the Business Reasons Behind a Diversity Training Request

Diversity Training project initiatives can be generated from a wide variety of sources. Often they will be generated because the organization has an opportunity that it would like to take advantage of or a specific problem that must be solved. At this point, you have received a request either to develop a performance solution or to determine why a performance problem exists. Someone could have even assumed that the solution requires diversity training before all of the facts are in. Nonetheless, the first step in the Needs Analysis process is to analyze this request.

"Solution" in this context means a system for resolving a performance problem; the solution may combine methods such as training, incentives, or process improvements. A solution encompasses an intervention, which is a specific event that is implemented to close a performance gap. "Performance problem" refers to performance that is not meeting expected outcomes or producing expected results (Barksdale and Lund, 2001). From a diversity point of view, it means determining that the performance related issue is one in which an improvement in diversity and inclusion skills, knowledge, competence, and abilities are required to address the issue.

If the request is to develop a specific solution, you must determine if there is a need to take a step back and look more closely at the proposed solution. Together with the internal business partner or requestor, you should determine why the diversity solution is needed and if the one proposed really is the best solution to meet the performance and/or business needs.

If the request is to determine why a performance problem exists, your job will be a bit easier, because the requester likely is already educated about the value of analysis and will be a cooperative partner in its completion. At the very least, the business partner who makes such a request already recognizes that a closer look at the problem needs to be taken and examine why it exists.

It is possible that you may be the one who becomes aware of the problem and brings it to the organization's attention and identifies the need for analysis. If this is the case, you will need to discuss the advantages of intervention options, such as diversity training, as a potential remedy. Regardless how the request is initiated, six key questions should be answered following the request:

1. What is the request, and why is it being made?

2. What is the urgency of the request?

3. What information needs to be collected and analyzed to design or procure the correct solution?

4. How closely is the request linked to the business?

5. What outcomes are expected, and are they clear?

6. What is the impact of the request on a diverse workforce or customer market (adapted from Barksdale and Lund, 2001)?

If these questions are not answered up front and quickly, the potential exists for wasting your time in needless activities or getting bogged down in useless detail resulting in a long, drawn out analysis. Knowing the answers to these questions will help you position your response to the request and help you determine if an analysis really is needed. Even if the analysis is completed quickly, it is a waste of time if conducting it is unnecessary.

At the end of this step you will know

► The information that needs to be gathered and how to get it quickly

► The information you have and how to validate it quickly

► How big the analysis is (the scope)

► Who your stakeholders are

► The expected outcomes for the solution

► The content of your Needs Analysis action plan.

In needs analysis, your goal is to determine the exact nature of the problem, its causes, and what to do about it. (Barksdale and Lund, 2001)

Very often, you will not have to do an extensive analysis or answer all these questions. Sometimes, a "quick-and-dirty" analysis will suffice to establish the cause(s) of the need. As with everything else, your approach will depend on circumstances: time, money, human resources, complexity of the problem, and criticality of solving it. While you may or may not need to perform an extensive analysis, you must answer the kinds of questions shown

What is the *background?*

- Who made the request?

- What led to the request?

- What groups/organizations are affected?

- Who needs training (if justified)?

What is the *performance discrepancy?*

- What are the details?

- What are the performance inputs?

- What are the performance outputs?

- What is the expected performance (standards)?

- What is the actual performance?

- What is the discrepancy's cost or effect?

- How important is it?

- How reliable is the evidence?

Is an effective *feedback system* involved?

- Do performers get regular feedback?

- How do performers receive feedback?

- Do performers know what to do, how to do it, and when to do it?

- Is feedback related to the task/function?

- Is feedback related to the specific required behavior or attitude needed?

- Is feedback provided in a timely fashion?

Are *motivational/incentive* factors involved?

- Does doing it right lead to a favorable outcome for the employee?

- Is the effort to perform well greater than the reward?

- Is doing it right somehow self-punishing?

- Is there an unfavorable outcome for poor performance?

- Is there pressure not to perform?

- Are there rewards for poor performance?

- Is punishment used as a management technique?

- Are standards of performance conflicting, unclear, or nonexistent?

- Is self-pride associated with doing the diversity and inclusion task?

- Does doing the work provide status rewards?

Are *job/organization design* factors involved?

- Do competing responsibilities prevent good performance?

- Does lack of accountability prevent good performance?

- Is there a lack of proper methods/procedures?

- Is there strong disagreement over the proper method/procedure/behavior?

- Can the job or role requirements be changed to improve performance?

- Is there a clear-cut organizational/reporting structure, chain of command, and work flow?

- Do conflicting interpretations of the corporate policy prevent required behavior or action?

Are *environmental factors* involved?

- Is there a lot of "downtime"?

- Must personnel wait around for a required output of another person/work function/machine/system?

- Are there many work distractions (for example telephone ringing, excess traffic flow through work space)?

- Is the environment a mess?

- Is new, unfamiliar equipment being used?

- Are furniture, tools, equipment, and supplies arranged conveniently and safely?

- Are tools and equipment adequate?

- Is there enough work space?

- Is lighting adequate?

- Is heating/ventilation adequate?

Is a lack of *skill or knowledge* involved?

- Do performers know how or when to do the work?

- Could performers do the work if their lives depended on it?

- Were they able to perform successfully in the past?

- Have they forgotten how?

- Does performance require skills that must be acquired through drill or practice?

- Is on-the-job speed so critical that it precludes use of a job aid or reference materials?

- What major job tasks/functions are affected?

Who are the *learners*?

- Can you identify jobs/job titles affected?

- Can you identify total numbers of personnel in each job or areas affected?

- Can you assess the background experience of each person in terms of:

    ▶ Training?

► Education?

► Job experience?

- Can learner attitudes/feelings toward the discrepancy, topic, or issue be described?

- Can learner attitudes toward training be described?

Using a Quick-and-Dirty Diversity Needs Analysis Approach

Even in a "quick-and-dirty" Diversity Training Needs Analysis, you will still need to complete the following steps:

1. Validate the request

2. Determine the background information needed

3. Identify the business need for the analysis

4. Identify the expected outcomes for the solution

5. Analyze the risks involved in conducting the analysis

6. Gain commitment to conduct the analysis

7. Clarify the information needed from the analysis based on the type of request

8. Determine the information you have and what you need

9. Define specific information

10. Develop a Diversity Training Needs Analysis project plan.

Maintaining the rigor involved in this approach will ensure that you cover all bases to develop a firm foundation for any DROI®-based conclusions you generate later in the Diversity Training evaluation process.

Validate the Request

Once you have received the request or after you have initiated the contact, it is your job to contact the requester to clarify what is being requested, to determine who and what is behind the request, and to assess its level of urgency. This information may be revealed automatically during the initial contact with the requester or may require a callback or short in-person meeting. It may require no meeting at all if you already are knowledgeable about the requester and the situation. Let's assume that you need a brief telephone meeting with the requester because you are unfamiliar with the situation. In this meeting it is important that at least two things happen:

- You gather and validate as much information as possible about the request as quickly as possible

- You communicate to the requester what key actions you will take as a result of the request.

The information you need to gather and validate from the requester includes the following:

- What is the request?

- What specifically are you being asked to do?

- What is the requester's role?

- Is the requester a sponsor, a stakeholder, a business partner, or someone other than the person who contacted you?

- What or who is driving the request? For example, is the requester grasping at straws to boost productivity or reduce costs or being forced to contact you because his or her manager thinks it is a good idea, or is there real commitment to solving a performance problem using the professional expertise you provide?

- What is the urgency of the request?

- When does the requester expect the analysis and solution to be completed?

- Is he or she aware of the time it will take to get to the finished product?

- If the request is extremely urgent, why? What has changed in the business that is making the performance problem critical? If the request is not urgent, then why is it being made?

- What is the risk of not responding to the request?

- What does the requester stand to gain or lose from the outcome of this request? Ultimately, what's in it for him or her to solve the performance problem? If the requester has no stake in the outcomes the solution is supposed to deliver, then it is doubtful that you will gain enough commitment to conduct an analysis, let alone develop a solution.

- Who will work with you to identify critical information, including business drivers, expected outcomes, available resources, and associated risks?

The following table provides more detail about the information you need regarding the request.

Table 4-1

Gathering and Validating Information	
Information Needed	**Rationale**
What is the request?	· To clarify what you are being asked to provide so you know how to respond. Perhaps the person is requesting a solution for which a program already exists, or he or she may be requesting analysis of a problem that is not a performance improvement problem. · To clarify the breadth, depth, desired results, and immediacy of the request.
Who is requesting the solution or analysis of a performance problem?	· To identify who, which often leads to why, is the critical thing to discover in this activity? You will also want to know what each person's level of authority and influence are so you will know if you have to go further up in the organization to sell the analysis and gain support. · Is the requester the sponsor? If not, who is? Will the requester provide the funding for the analysis and the solution? · To clarify the role and authority of the requester.
Who else is involved?	· To determine who the other stakeholders are (assuming the requester is one), who your business partners are, and who your customers are. · To determine who else has a significant role in this request.

Gathering and Validating Information	
Information Needed	**Rationale**
What or who is behind the request?	· To assess whether the request is being made due to a change in business drivers or some other organizational change or whether it is personality driven. This information will make a big difference in how you respond to and approach the analysis. · To determine if there is a hidden agenda. · To determine what is prompting the request and why.
What is the urgency of the request?	· To determine why the request is being made now-what has changed in the business? · To determine requester expectations for delivery of the solution. · To determine the time frame of the request for the analysis and the design of the solution.
What will this person stand to gain or lose from solving the performance problem?	· To determine why the request is being made and to begin to assess commitment to analyzing the performance problem. · To identify the risk tolerance of the requester for a correct and incorrect solution (the lower the tolerance of risk, the greater the importance of analysis).
Who will work with you to identify critical information?	· To make certain someone is available and responsible to help identify information needed.

Source: Rapid Needs Analysis, Barksdale and Lund, 2001

The key actions you will take in response to the request should be communicated to the requester during this meeting. They should include the following:

- An analysis most likely will be required if the request is to develop a solution. The analysis will help determine if the solution will meet business and performance needs through the desired outcomes.

- The analysis can be completed quickly-sometimes in as few as 10 days.

- The analysis will be done with help from the requester.

- Just because an analysis has been conducted does not mean that the solution identified by the requester will be the solution recommended.

- If the requested solution or performance problem identification is not urgent, is not linked to business needs, or lacks management commitment, there probably is no need to conduct an analysis or develop a solution.

- The work environment will be respected during the analysis, and as little disruption as possible will take place.

- Analysis is the first step of solution design, and gathering information will ensure effective and efficient design that will not need to be reworked.

Whether conducted in person or by telephone, this validation meeting is critical in establishing the need for and importance of the analysis and helps position the additional fact finding you will do in this step as a way to determine if an analysis will be conducted.

Determine the Background Information Needed

As stated earlier, the first activity in identifying the overall scope of the project is gathering background information. You will need information about the following factors:

▶ *How the problem links to the business* — This helps validate and determine extent and breadth of the problem and its importance to the organization

▶ *The specific desired outcomes for the solution* — Identifies the type of information regarding the performance problem and the solution parameters.

▶ *The resources needed for the analysis* — You depend on others to help you gather information that is vital to an accurate analysis. Resources could include data from human resource, cultural audit, and customer information systems, *etc.*

▶ *The risk involved in the project* — The higher the risk of the solution being incomplete or "wrong," the more information that must be gathered and the more detailed the analysis must be.

▶ *Who needs to commit to the analysis?* — This helps to identify the number of people whose commitment is required to move the Diversity Training initiative forward and sustain it (adapted from Barksdale and Lund, 2001).

Identify the Business Need for the Analysis

An important component of a needs analysis is linking the

performance need to the organization's business drivers and business needs. A clear understanding of how the solution links to the business makes it possible for you to decrease steps or take shortcuts in the analysis and still ensure that the solution resulting from the analysis will meet its expected outcomes. (Barksdale and Lund, 2001)

"Business drivers" are the external and internal factors that drive an organization's strategy and therefore its business and performance needs. External business drivers are outside of an organization's control and typically include the following:

▶ *Economic drivers* include upturns or downturns in the economy, embargoes or trade restrictions, and other economically driven situations.

▶ *Human resource drivers* include shortages of resources or of certain skills, union demands or contracts, and employee needs to balance family and work relationships.

▶ *Government drivers*, such as regulations or deregulation, force changes in competition or the environment as a whole.

▶ *Public perception drivers* involve the public's view of the organization. This view may be influenced by press coverage of an event or situation that arose outside of the organization's control.

▶ *Market or customer drivers* include increased competition or other changes in how the organization views the marketplace in which it competes, as well as changes in customer demographics, definition, and needs that place demands on products or necessitate changes in product design.

Internal business drivers are generated by internal decisions. Sometimes an internal business driver is a response to an external business driver. There typically is a stakeholder inside of the organization for this type of driver. Internal drivers include the following:

▶ *Technology drivers* are new innovations and technology that create opportunities or needs for changes in information keeping and processing.

▶ *Changes in system, process, or key policy drivers* change employee skill or behavior requirements.

▶ *Shareholder or financial drivers* include Wall Street or bank demands for higher profits or lower costs to which the organization must respond.

▶ *New product generation drivers* are market or customer changes that result in new or revised products or services to meet demand or need. (Barksdale and Lund, 2001)

An organization identifies business needs, and corresponding objectives and strategies, to respond to business drivers. For example, if the business driver is increased competition, a business need may be to use diverse work team creativity to improve current products or create new products and services. The performance need defines what individual employees must achieve to address the business driver and support the corresponding business need. For example, if increasing market share was an identified business driver, a business need may be to begin to sell products and services to customers in emerging multicultural markets where the organization has little or no experience or skill.

The performance need identified is to increase the sales staff's product knowledge and recognition of which products within the product family complement each other and are potential prospects for a particular emerging market customer base. Performance needs usually drive a performance solution. The same performance needs define the value of the solution to the organization and justify the organization's investment in it. Performance needs are also referred to as "expected performance" or "expected outcomes." This fact alone highlights why it is essential to identify these "expected performance items" or "expected outcomes" at the outset of the Diversity Training Needs analysis process.

By identifying and linking business drivers to performance needs, you will be able to show how the requested solution will address the performance needs, business needs, and ultimately the business drivers. This alignment to the business is critical. The tool shown below can help demonstrate this linkage.

Table 4-2

Diversity Alignment Matrix: Aligning Diversity Training Initiatives with Business Drivers			
Potential Solution	**Performance Need**	**Business Need**	**Business Driver**
Training on multicultural customer knowledge and buying preferences	Increase sales force and employee knowledge of cultural competencies required to sell in emerging markets	To increase share of wallet in emerging markets	Potential loss of market share in emerging markets and overall market performance (competition) (external driver)

Adapted from: Rapid Needs Analysis, Barksdale and Lund, 2001

Identify the Expected Outcomes for the Solution

Now that you have identified the business drivers and linked them to the requested solution, you will need to identify the expected outcomes of the solution. It is important to clarify what the requester hopes to accomplish through the performance solution. What does he or she want the audience to do as a result of the solution? Examples of outcomes are "resolve cross-cultural conflicts in a respectful and inclusive way," "to reduce turnover among high potential women and minorities," "to decrease design time for new products using diverse work teams," or "to decrease the time to market in emerging market segments."

During this stage of the Diversity Training Needs Analysis process, a wide variety of outcomes may be identified. It is helpful to begin with a list of the top 5-6 outcomes and briefly outline their importance to the organization. These outcomes will provide the framework for your analysis and ultimately will be used to identify the objectives and measures for the solution itself.

The outcomes identified must be:

- ▶ Realistic-Are they sound? Do they make sense'?

- ▶ Business related-Are they related to the business needs and ultimately business drivers?

- ▶ Measurable-Can they be measured so the solution's success can be evaluated?

- ▶ Achievable-Are they achievable given the current business environment?

If the requester is not able to identify outcomes, try to determine why not? Is the business need still unclear? Is the requested or potential solution off track? Is the problem not really a performance or role or behavior problem? If so, work with the requestor and key stakeholders to determine the type of issue and identify the appropriate solution. The real solution may not involve training at all. The matrix below contains a process that can be used to work through the identification of outcomes with the requester. It should look familiar, because it has all of the elements of the Diversity Alignment Matrix, but the columns are reversed to start with the business driver and work back to the outcomes. Identifying outcomes in this way will help you ensure they are aligned with the business drivers and goals.

Table 4-3

Outcome Identification Matrix: Aligning Business Drivers with Initiative Outcomes				
Business Driver	**Business Need**	**Performance Need**	**Potential Solution**	**Initiative Outcomes**
Potential loss of market share in emerging markets and overall market performance (competition) (external driver)	To increase share of wallet in emerging markets	Increase sales force and employee knowledge of cultural competencies required to sell in emerging markets	Training on multicultural customer knowledge and buying preferences	To be able to sell against competitors' products in emerging markets To use customer cultural background information during a sales call

Adapted from: *Rapid Needs Analysis*, Barksdale and Lund, 2001

Analyze the Risks Involved in Conducting the Analysis

During the risk analysis, you will need to answer questions such as the following:

▶ What will happen if the performance problem is not solved?

▶ Will there be any impact at all on the business?

▶ If there is no impact on the business, then why solve the problem?

- ► What is the risk involved in not providing a solution to the problem?

There are a number of risk factors involved in conducting the analysis. Some of these factors may include:

- ► Reasons for the request

- ► Commitment of sponsors

- ► Clarity of business drivers

- ► Level of urgency

- ► Alignment of proposed or potential solution with business need

- ► Alignment of proposed or potential solution with expected outcomes

- ► Business linkage

- ► Availability of information needed

- ► Availability of funding

- ► Availability of human resources required

- ► Potential environmental barriers to solution's success

- ► Stability of environment (*i.e.*, will the environment change before the solution can be implemented?)

- ► Level of commitment needed from those who will be involved in providing information for the analysis

After you have identified potential risks that exist in conducting a Diversity Training Needs Analysis you should know if an analysis is warranted. If you identify more than three or four risk factors, you may want to reconsider the training project as a candidate for a "quick and dirty" Needs Analysis. A more detailed analysis will be required. You will also want to know what happens if you do not do an analysis or agree to the requester's initial request. The results of each of these options will provide valuable information to bring the analysis to a successful conclusion.

Gain Commitment to Conduct the Analysis

Once you have made the decision to recommend a needs analysis to your business partners (requestors), you must gain their commitment to complete it. If you have gathered the information identified and discussed up to this point, there should be no surprises. Before you ask for commitment to the analysis, it is helpful to take a quick inventory of the information you have gathered regarding the request up to this point.

This information should include:

- ▶ Identity of the requester

- ▶ Identity of the sponsors

- ▶ Identity of other key players who have an interest in the performance problem

- ▶ General description of the targeted audience

- ▶ Description of the performance improvement need as identified by the requester

- ▶ Determination of whether or not the problem really is a performance problem

- ▶ Project scope

- ▶ Project urgency

- ▶ Potential project risks

- ▶ Expected outcomes for the solution

You should now have a good feel for whether you will have the support needed from management to conduct the analysis and eventually design and develop the solution. If you encounter resistance at this point, most likely you will have to gather additional information to find out why. Perhaps some information was missing from your initial analysis of the request or a key person was missing from the meetings. Some issues to consider if you run into resistance include the following:

- ▶ Identify who has the most to gain or lose from the DTROI® study. How will the results affect them; how will they benefit from the study'?

- ▶ Find out not only who does not agree with conducting the analysis, but why. Become knowledgeable about time and money constraints and the politics surrounding the situation.

- ▶ Articulate the performance need in business terms, and state the benefits of the analysis as related to business results. Selling the need for the analysis by emphasizing its benefits is particularly effective if done from the client's perspective — what's in it for them to have the analysis completed?

▶ Being clear about the consequences of not conducting an analysis will help you gain commitment to it. Consequences may include spending money on the wrong performance intervention, developing a solution that is outmoded in the current environment, or alienating the audience with irrelevant training (Barksdale and Lund, 2001).

Although the commitment you receive at this point is verbal, it is recommended that you get written agreement, or "signoff," to conduct the analysis when you present the project plan to the requester, sponsor, and stakeholders. It is entirely possible that you will decide not to conduct the analysis. If this is the case, it is your responsibility to contact the requester and those involved in the process and to be as candid as possible about why you made that decision.

Clarify the Information Needed from the Analysis based on the Type of Request

It is imperative to clarify the type of information that is needed from the analysis based on the type of request that has been made. It requires that you target the data collection efforts to validate the request and analyze how to address the performance gap. The following highlight a few examples of the types of requests you may receive:

▶ Resolve communication conflicts which occur among

diverse work groups. The requester may want your help to improve the organization's work climate by building cross-cultural communication skill development among employees.

▶ Implement a new multicultural marketing process or process change. The requester typically asks for your help in redesigning a process, such as streamlining a diverse customer telemarketing rapport building method during the ordering process or training diverse work groups in utilizing their differences to enhance creativity and innovation to decrease the time it takes to design a new emerging market product before it goes to manufacturing.

▶ Build an identified skill need. The requester says, "We have identified a need for employees to have the ability to…." The requester is specific about what type of proficiency is needed, and your job is to determine how to develop the proficiency using diversity techniques and strategies.

▶ Develop an identified knowledge need. The requester has identified a knowledge gap and requests that you develop employees' "information base." For example, the employee needs to "recall" or "translate" information related to utilizing cultural competence when handling community-based situations. You need to determine how to transfer the knowledge to the employee in a way that can be applied in these critical reputation building situations.

▶ Presented with a defined performance gap. The requester defines the performance gap but not whether it is a specific skill or knowledge deficiency (or some combination). For this type of request, you must identify what the audience needs to meet the desired performance before you can develop a solution or intervention.

▶ Given a predefined solution or intervention. The requester has the "fix" in mind, such as "We need Company XYZ's Diversity training course" or "We need diverse work group team building or diversity leadership or another kind of training." In this case you first need to validate the performance problem and desired outcomes, and then you need to determine if the requester's solution is the correct one-all without creating a political nightmare!

▶ Need a job aid or behavioral support tool. The requester makes a specific request for assistance with a specific behavioral issue that is diversity-related. The information needed is reasonably clear, and your job is to determine the format for presentation or delivery of the content in some sort of tool. You recognize components that can be addressed with a job aid or support tool. (Nonetheless, it is still important to implement all of the steps to validate the need and identify the correct solution(s)).

▶ An unidentified performance gap for a defined business need. The business need has been identified (e.g., sales need to increase revenue in emerging markets, errors need to decrease, diverse customer complaints need to be resolved), but the how, what, and who may not be clearly defined.

The table below highlights a few approaches to collect data to address a Requestor's needs:

Table 4-4

Type of Request	Information Needed from Analysis	Potential Activities for Gathering Information
New process or process change	• What the process is (*e.g.*, step outline, outputs) • Who will be affected by the change and how • A comparison of the old environment with the new environment • How the process change will be implemented • Documentation or supporting materials that define the new process (and old process if it is a change) • Identification of environmental issues • Data to support performance problem • Listing of previous programs • Audience information	• Focus groups and interviews (minimum one week for script and interview development and facilitation to assess perspectives, expectations, and so forth. • Observations of current environment to assess change. (minimum three days) • Review documentation (minimum two days)
Identified skill need	• Definition of the skill (*e.g.*, what is "overcomes resistance"?) • Definition of the current skill level (or if skill even exists in desired populations) • Definition of desired skill outputs • Identification of environmental issues • Data to support performance problem • listing of previous programs • Audience information	• Interviews with "skill experts" to define skill and expected outputs as well as required foundational skills (minimum one week for script and interview development and facilitation) • Focus groups or observations to gain input on skill level or foundation requirements (minimum one week)

Type of Request	Information Needed from Analysis	Potential Activities for Gathering Information
Identified knowledge need	· Definition of the knowledge (*e.g.*, what is "understands stereotypes and how they develop from cultural programming"?) · Definition of the current knowledge level (or if knowledge even exists in desired populations) · Definition of desired knowledge outputs · Identification of environmental issues · Data to support performance problem · Listing of previous programs · Audience information	· Interview "knowledge experts" to define knowledge and expected outputs as well as required foundational knowledge (minimum one week for script and interview development and facilitation) · Focus groups or observations to gain input on knowledge level or foundation requirements (minimum one week)
New system or system change	· System specifications · Projection of performance needs (skill and knowledge) · Projection of process changes · Assessment of job impact · Identification of environmental issues · Data to support performance problem · Listing of previous programs · Audience information	· Review of documentation (specifications and projections) (minimum three days) · Observations or focus groups (minimum one week)
Defined performance gap	· Assessment of current environment against desired outcomes to identify skill or knowledge gap · Identification of environmental issues · Data to support performance problem · Listing of previous programs · Audience information	· Focus groups or interviews to gain perception of performance need and resistance to gap identification or change (minimum one week) · Observations to validate gap and determine skill or knowledge requirements (minimum two weeks)

Type of Request	Information Needed from Analysis	Potential Activities for Gathering Information
Predefined solution or intervention	· Validation of request against audience perception · Identification of environmental issues · Data to support performance problem · Listing of previous programs · Audience information	· Focus groups or interviews (minimum one week)
Job aid	· Review of documentation or information needed · Audience preferences for design · Identification of environmental issues · Data to support performance problem · Listing of previous programs · Audience information	· Documentation review (minimum one day) · Interviews or focus groups (minimum one week)
Unidentified performance gap-defined business need	· Organization information · Identification of best practice information · Identification of environmental issues · Data to support performance problem · Listing of previous programs · Audience information	· Literature search (minimum two days) · Organizational background research (minimum two days) · Survey (optional) (minimum two weeks) · Focus groups (minimum one week) · Observations (minimum three days)

Adapted from: Rapid Needs Analysis, Barksdale and Lund, 2001

As you become more skilled in the Needs Assessment data collection process, you will develop your own tips, tools, approaches and experience which you can catalogue for future reference. In addition, list key questions and the responses you get to form an assessment resource data and knowledge-base. This will be especially useful when you develop the final DTROI® report.

Determine the Information You Have and What You Need

You need to collect information to identify the current situation. Some of this information you already may have from analyzing the request, and some of it you will need to collect by going out to the environment. This may be as easy as sending an email message to one of your identified resources, or it can be as complex as getting funding approval to establish a new Assistant Diversity Director position. Keep in mind that the amount of information gathered will affect the amount of analysis required and, ultimately, the amount of time it takes to complete the next step in the process. Key to the Diversity Needs Analysis process is focusing on the information most critical to determining the performance problem or opportunity and getting to the "right" solution. As mentioned previously, the solution may or may not involve Diversity training.

Key categories of information to be collected might include the following:

Organizational information:

- ▶ strategic plans
- ▶ mission statements

- goals and objectives

- organization charts

- descriptions of major initiatives

- *etc.*

Best practice information (based upon proven ROI returns to the business):

- DROI® leaders in the industry (what are their DROI® practices, and what they did to achieve their measurable DROI® results?)

- leaders in developing state-of-the-art performance solutions

Past and current programs that address identified diversity-related performance problems or opportunities:

- training

- processes

- systems

- other initiatives

Audience information:

- who

- how many

- location

- education level

- experience level

- current job knowledge

- current job skills

- current job performance

- current job attitudes

- physical conditions of the work area

- nature and extent of supervision

- position descriptions

- others who influence or support the targeted audience

- performance plans

- *etc.*

Environmental issues:

- constraints

- politics

- cultural factors

- economic factors

- *etc.*

Business-related Data to support performance problem and expected outcomes:

- ▶ performance results

- ▶ customer feedback

- ▶ lost revenue

- ▶ increased costs

- ▶ attrition rates

- ▶ *etc.*

There are a number of questions you should pose as you gather your research information (ponder on your own), conduct interviews or focus groups (ask others), design or implement surveys (ask yourself and others), or review documentation or background information (ask yourself and others).

Table 4-5

Defining Specific Information	
Information to Gather	**Question or Probe**
Organizational information	· How would the intervention or solution support the organization's strategy or initiative? · Is this type of request in alignment with the organization's goals and objectives? · What is the "span of influence" of this request (who would be affected, and how? · Does or will the request support a major initiative, or is it in conflict with a major initiative? · How would the organization benefit if the requested solution or intervention is successful? How would you know?

Defining Specific Information	
Information to Gather	**Question or Probe**
Best DROI® practices information	· Who is seen as a best practice organization for this type of request based upon true DROI® returns? What measureable evidence exist? · How is that organization different from yours? How is it the same? · What would have to change within your organization to mirror or exceed the DROI® best practices organization? · How would this change occur? · What constraints currently exist in your organization that may limit its ability to become a DROI® best practices organization? Why do these constraints exist?
Past and current programs that address identified performance problem	· What past or current programs address the request? · What past or current programs do you see as a foundation (or knowledge or skill builder) that support but do not meet the request? Why or how? · What percentage of the audience has participated in past or current programs? · What is not working or disliked about past or current programs? · What is working well or liked about past or current programs? · How do past or current programs relate to this request?
Audience information	· What is the audience's perception of the request (*e.g.,* problem, need, change)? · Is there resistance, and if so, what is it? · What does the audience see as the request? · What are the audience requirements or preferences that may influence the request (*e.g.,* no travel, face-to- face interaction) ? · What is a motivator for the audience to participate and implement the change that will result from the request? · What are the audience demographics? · What constraints exist for the audience?

Defining Specific Information	
Information to Gather	**Question or Probe**
Environmental issues	· What constraints exist in the environment that might limit the success of the request? · What is the environment? · Who has control over the environment, and what is their perception of the request? · How will the environment affect the request? What is the relationship of the environment to the request? · How has the environment influenced the need for the request?
Data to support performance problem and expected outcomes	· Is the request valid? · How does the performance information (perceived or actual) support or contradict the request? · Would these outcomes occur if the request were implemented? How would you know? · How would you know if the request were successful? · How would you know if the request were unsuccessful?

Adapted from: *Rapid Needs Analysis*, Barksdale and Lund, 2001

Spending time to review questions and probes such as these will help you take a comprehensive, strategic approach to the Diversity Needs Analysis task ensuring that you obtain the specific information that will be critical to a successful outcome.

Develop a Diversity Training Needs Analysis Report and Project Plan

One last activity remains in analyzing the request: developing the Diversity Training Needs Analysis Project Plan and Report. A project plan is necessary in communicating analysis responsibilities, timelines, and deliverables. Developing a written project plan and report is critical in Diversity Needs Analysis because of the amount of information that has to be collected and processed and the variety of people who will help collect it.

This report includes your plan of action as well as your findings and your recommendations. The needs analysis provides you with the information you require to decide whether or not training is the correct solution. The report offers written justification for your decision. The needs analysis report can also serve as a valuable source document for further course development activities. The report should have the main headings shown below however the items under each heading may vary from report to report. (Trainer's Library, AT&T, 1987)

Format for the Diversity Training Needs Analysis Report

Executive summary (optional)

A. Introduction to the report

- 1. Statement of the problems

- 2. How the project originated

- 3. Previous investigation

- 4. Procedures used to do the needs analysis

- 5. Definition of Diversity and Inclusion

- 6. EEO/affirmative action/Diversity and Inclusion Mission statement

- 7. DROI®/DROM® Business Case for Diversity

B. Findings

- Problems identified

- Performance problems

- Problems other than performance

- Causes of the problems

- Result (cost) of the problems

- Personnel affected by the problems

C. Possible solutions

- Description of solutions

- No action

- Action involving training

- Action not involving training

- Comparison of solutions

- Problems associated with each solution

D. Recommended solution

- 1. Detailed description of solution

- 2. Rationale for choice

- 3. Population affected by solution

E. Project scope and schedule

- Description of project scope

- Description of project constraints

- Resources (people/time/money) required

- Estimated schedule

F. Appendixes

- Initial project requests

- Correspondence

- Cost of conducting needs analysis

- Data-gathering tools

- Raw data

Format for the Diversity Training Needs Analysis Project Plan

Analyzing the Request
Major Milestones

▶ Validate the request

▶ Determine what background information is needed

▶ Identify the business need for the analysis

- ▶ Identify the expected outcomes for the solution

- ▶ Analyze the risks involved in conducting the analysis

- ▶ Gain commitment to conduct the analysis

- ▶ Clarify information needed from the analysis based on the type of request

- ▶ Determine what information you have and what you need

- ▶ Define specific information

- ▶ Develop the Diversity Needs Analysis Project Plan

Time frame

1-2 days

Deliverables

- ▶ Recommendation to conduct (or not conduct) the analysis

- ▶ List of information to be gathered and how it will be gathered

- ▶ Outcomes expected from the solution

- ▶ Diversity Training Needs Analysis Project Plan

Investigating the Cause(s) of the Performance Problem

As mentioned previously, you will have to determine the primary cause(s) for the performance gap to see whether Diversity training is indicated or whether some other solution should be recommended. You will need to rely on the same key stakeholders such as the Requestor. Also, you should investigate any and all supporting documents that exist to help determine the cause(s) for what is happening. These include:

▶ Organization goals and objectives

▶ Methods and procedures

▶ Job and role descriptions

▶ System documentation

▶ Field complaints

▶ Existing job studies or skill studies

To locate the causes of the performance gap, you may also need to examine the backgrounds of the Learners. This includes taking advantage of the following kinds of data sources:

▶ General personnel records

▶ Training records

▶ Former instructors

▶ Corporate tests

▶ Supervisors

▶ Job history

▶ Learners themselves

► Customers

► *Etc.*

When investigating the actual nature of the problem, you should make sure to ground your findings in truth. What you need is hard, objective proof, if it is available. This kind of data can be found by looking at *"critical incident reports"* the outcomes of performance and at records of the results of performance. Such data sources include:

► Actual job outputs

► Sales figures

► Customer or user letters-complimentary or complaining

► Records of employee turnover

► Cultural Audit and/or Engagement Survey Verbatim Comments

► Attendance records

► Safety records

► Records of exit interviews

► Any other quantitative records of performance

► Any other descriptive records of performance.

Your discussions with managers, supervisors, job performers, and others may suggest further sources of objective data. Pursue them in addition to those listed.

Subjective Data Sources for Gathering Data

You will also need to interview various people, either directly or through questionnaires, for their perception of the problem. Such people include:

- ▶ Managers/supervisors
- ▶ Master job or role performers or performers of skills
- ▶ The person requesting training
- ▶ Users of job/role/skill outputs
- ▶ Subject-matter experts
- ▶ Methods personnel
- ▶ Measurements and results personnel
- ▶ Job/position designers

Final Thoughts

The Diversity Needs and Requirements Analysis phase of the Diversity Training Return on Investment process requires acute attention to detail and will require time and effort. Nonetheless, by taking the time to conduct a thorough analysis, you will significantly reduce the risk of a failed program with little or no real measurable impact. Think of it as insurance against developing the wrong or an unneeded solution. By gathering information using these techniques and processes, you will build a thorough understanding of the context in which the performance must take place to be successful and a credible basis upon which to calculate your Diversity Return on Investment (DROI®).

References

AT&T, *The Trainers Library*, Evaluation, Massachusetts: Addison-Wesley Publishing, 1987.

Barksdale, S., and Lund, T., *Rapid Needs Analysis*, ASTD Press, 2001.

Fisher, Sharon G., Ruffino, Barbara J., *Establishing the Value of Training*, HRD Press, 1996

Hodell, Chuck, American Society for Training & Development *ISD from the Ground Up*, ASTD Press, 2000.

Hubbard, Edward E., *How to Calculate Diversity Return on Investment.* California: Global Insights Publishing, 1999.

Hubbard, Edward E., *The Diversity Scorecard: Evaluating the Impact of Diversity on Organizational Performance.* Massachusetts: Butterworth-Heinemann, Elsevier Publishing, 2004.

Hubbard, Edward E., *The Diversity Discipline: Implementing Diversity Work with a Strategy, Structure, and ROI Measurement Focus.* California: Global Insights Publishing, 2009.

Plummer, Deborah L., *Handbook of Diversity Management.* Maryland: University Press of America, Inc. 2003

CHAPTER 5

Diversity Training Evaluation Tools

Creating Diversity Training Evaluation Measurement Tools

Introduction

Skills development is one of several activities that must be undertaken to achieve an organization's strategic diversity objectives. As mentioned earlier, the only way to determine that diversity training and skills development are having the desired effect is to use formal training evaluation processes and cost-benefit analysis methods. The results of these activities can confirm the positive effects of training and development and identify improvements to make it better. Evaluation can contribute to maximizing the organization's return on training investment.

This chapter illustrates evaluation tools and approaches that can be used to determine how well the diversity training intervention delivered on its stated learning and performance objectives and strategic outcomes.

Evaluation

Remember, evaluation means to measure something in preparation for making a decision: for example, to stop, modify, or expand it to increase its benefits. This implies:

▶ Knowing what decision the evaluation data will help you make.

▶ Measuring scientifically, using data collection methods and research designs that separate the effects your program is having from all other influences on your outcome variables.

▶ Choosing the right measures for what your program is really trying to accomplish.

Evaluation efforts throughout this book can be described as formative or summative. Formative means evaluation data are used to see how a program is doing, to modify it or improve it. Summative means data are used to make a final judgment on a program: it worked or it didn't, was or was not worth its cost, should be continued or dropped.

Types of Skill Development Measures

It is useful first to distinguish results measures from other types of measures commonly used to evaluate human resource programs.

In a famous article, Kirkpatrick observed that training and other programs could be evaluated at one of four levels: reaction, learning, behavior, results. Building on this model, Jack Phillips added a fifth level: return on investment. A summary of the model levels is shown below:

Table 5-1

Kirkpatrick Skills Evaluation Model Plus	
Level	**Description**
Level 1: Reaction	How people feel (reactions) about the diversity skills development program and what do they plan to do with the material?
Level 2: Learning	Whether people know anything as a result of the diversity skills development program. What skills, knowledge, or attitudes have changed and by how much?
Level 3: Behavior	Whether people do anything differently after the diversity skills development program. Did participants apply on the job what they learned?
Level 4: Results	Hard outcome measures of individual or organizational effectiveness produced by the diversity skills development program. Did the on-the-job application of this program produce measurable results?
Level 5: Return-on-Training Investment	Financial results of the diversity skills development program. Did the monetary value of the results exceed the cost for the program?

Caution! The four levels of evaluation should be used in sequence. It is acceptable to use Levels 1 and 2 by themselves. Levels 3 and 4 should not normally be used unless you have positive results from a Level 2 evaluation. Without a Level 2 evaluation, it is difficult to relate the results of Level 3 evaluation back to training. This is because factors other than training can influence on-the-job transfer. If you do a Level 3 without a Level 2, you need to rule out these other factors before you can assume that training had positive or negative outcomes. With Level 4 evaluation, it is important to have some evidence of training results at both the learning and transfer levels. Once this is accomplished, you can begin to explore the cost-benefit, return-on-investment relationship that ties the Diversity training effort to the bottom-line.

How Much Training Evaluation Do You Need?

Anyone responsible for diversity training is also responsible for evaluation. The amount of evaluation that you provide depends on the types of decisions that your organization must make and the information needed to make those decisions. For example, if your only requirement is to ensure that participants have positive attitudes toward the course, then Level 1 evaluation is sufficient. But, if your goal is to determine whether your diversity course is having a positive effect on job performance, then you will have to do Level 3 evaluation, and this means that you will also have to do Level 1 and 2. They provide the basis for determining whether participants want to use what they have learned and have indeed learned the appropriate attitudes and skills.

Where Do You Begin?

Your first step in evaluating diversity training is to determine your major evaluation questions. The second step is to use the relevant sections of this chapter to plan and conduct the appropriate level of training evaluation. The following decision table may help you identify some of the major questions and methods:

Table 5-2

Major Questions	Evaluation Technique
How satisfied are the participants with the course?	**Level 1:** Reaction evaluation
Do the participants believe that they learned the values and skills that the course was intended to teach?	**Level 2:** Learning evaluation. Use the learning self-assessment evaluation tool.
Can the participants demonstrate the values, knowledge, and skills that are taught in the course?	**Level 2:** Learning evaluation. Use the short-answer evaluation tool.
Do the participants report that they are using their diversity values, knowledge, and skills on the job?	**Level 3:** Behavior evaluation. Use the post-training survey for course participants.
Do the managers of the participants have the impression that the participants are using their diversity values, knowledge, and skills on the job?	**Level 3:** Behavior evaluation. Use the post-training survey for managers of participants. For example, the manager fills out a survey based on general impressions of the participant.
Do the managers actually observe and report that participants are using their Diversity values, knowledge, and skills on the job?	**Level 3:** Behavior evaluation. Use the Diversity behavior checklist. For example, the manager keeps a record of observations for one month.
Do managers believe that the organization is benefiting from diversity training?	**Level 4:** Results evaluation. Use the organizational results questionnaire tool.

Major Questions	Evaluation Technique
Does the organization experience specific benefits (financial and non-financial) as a result of the diversity training program?	**Level 5:** Return-on-Investment evaluation. Use the diversity cost and benefit formulas and calculations.

As we explore each diversity training evaluation level, we will answer the following questions:

▶ What is this technique?

▶ When is it used?

▶ What measures are available using this level?

Level 1: Participant Reactions

What Is This Technique?

The purpose of Level 1 evaluation of participants reactions is to find out how the learners feel about the training. It provides a measure of customer satisfaction that is useful for determining whether learners have a positive attitude toward the course and how to improve it if they do not.

The intent of this initial level of evaluation is to measure participant' attitudes and feelings toward:

▶ interest and usefulness of the content

- ► effectiveness of the instructor

- ► quality of the materials

This level of evaluation does not tell you how much participants learned (the learning level does this). However, this level is important because it provides you with continuous feedback for quality improvement. It also provides a forum for participants to air their suggestions, and it helps you produce a course that is satisfying as well as effective.

When Is It Used?

Level 1 evaluation is used for almost every training event. A Level 1 questionnaire can be given to the participants at several different times:

- ► **End of course.** Having participants fill out the Level 1 measure at the end of the training session while they are still in the classroom is the most common approach.

- ► **During the course.** It can also be given at the end of each day during a multiple day program. This gives the instructor and course manager valuable information that can be used to confirm that the course is on the right track or to determine what changes to make the next day. Daily evaluations are useful if you have more than one instructor or speaker. They allow the participants to respond while their reactions are still fresh.

▶ **Shortly after the course.** If it is not feasible to do a Level 1 evaluation while participants are still in the classroom, they can do it within a short time after the course and return it by mail. However, this is less desirable because of uncontrollable factors that can influence responses, and some participants usually do not return questionnaires.

What measures are available using this level?

There are two approaches: one for rating scales and one for open-ended questions.

Rating scales: For each question, add the individual responses and divide by the total number of responses to find the average. This is the most common and useful statistic.

$$= \frac{\# \text{ individual responses}}{\text{total responses}}$$

If you want more detail, you can add the total number of each type of response (how many people answered "1." how many answered "2," *etc.*). This is called a frequency distribution, and it gives you a picture of how similar or different people's attitudes are.

There are other statistics that can be computed, and they are described in other technical books and materials on evaluation. The two described here are sufficient for most purposes.

The scores from the rating scale provide a quantitative measure that is easy to use for making comparisons between individuals or courses.

Each item has a scale ranging from 1 for poor to 5 for excellent. There are also short-answer questions that ask about major strengths, suggestions for improvement, and general comments.

The advantages of the tool in this section is that it can be administered quickly; the process of analyzing participant responses can be automated by using scanning equipment and statistical software packages (such as Hubbard & Hubbard, Inc. "20/20 Insight Gold Survey Analysis Software." It compiles both rating scale and open-ended response data items); and you can compare the results of one course to another. The disadvantage is that it does not give you very much information about the specifics of the course content, goals, instructor, or materials.

Open-ended questions: To analyze the results, you will summarize the answers that participants have given. If it is a small class and the answers are short, you can simply list them in your summary of class activity. When the class is large, or the answers are long, then the procedure is to read them and sort them into groups of similar comments or themes. For each group of similar comments, write a comment or paragraph that captures the key points. You can then list a few of the actual comments or excerpts as examples.

The second Level 1 tool contains items that ask about overall course and materials, instructor effectiveness, potential applications after training, and suggestions for improvement. Most of the items are open-ended, but a few have rating scales.

Variations. You can modify both of the tools discussed here by changing the contents to include the topics of most interest to you and to fit the time allocated for this evaluation. You can also modify the format of the tools by changing open-ended questions to rating scales and vice versa. It all depends on the amount and type of information that you want to receive.

The information that follows illustrates examples of a rating scale and open-ended measurement tool.

Figure 5-3

Reactions to Diversity Training

Instructions: For each, circle the number that represents your opinion.

Precourse Preparation

1. My level of understanding of the objectives and job relevance of this course before attending it

    1 - Poor   2 - Fair   3 - Good   4 - Very Good   5 - Excellent

Overall Course

2. Level of difficulty of the course

    1 - Poor   2 - Fair   3 - Good   4 - Very Good   5 - Excellent

3. The degree to which the course met my expectations

    1 - Poor   2 - Fair   3 - Good   4 - Very Good   5 - Excellent

Expectation for Job Transfer

1. Relevancy of the course to my job

    1 - Poor   2 - Fair   3 - Good   4 - Very Good   5 - Excellent

Materials/Media

1. Consistency of materials and media with course objectives

    1 - Poor   2 - Fair   3 - Good   4 - Very Good   5 - Excellent

Instructor Effectiveness

1. Instructor's ability to deal with conflict in a productive manner

    1 - Poor   2 - Fair   3 - Good   4 - Very Good   5 - Excellent

2. Instructor's ability to deal with emotional issues

    1 - Poor   2 - Fair   3 - Good   4 - Very Good   5 - Excellent

Short Answer

1. The most beneficial part of the course was:

2. The least beneficial part of the course was:

Figure 5-4

Participant Reactions: Open-Ended
Course Evaluation

Instructions: For those question items that use a rating scale, circle the number that best represents your opinion. For all other question items, write your response in the space provided.

Overall Course and Materials

1. Overall, this workshop was:

   1 - Poor   2 - Fair   3 - Good   4 - Very Good   5 - Excellent

2. What, if any, aspects of the training were distracting or inhibited your learning?

   _____

3. What did the training provide that you did not anticipate?

   _____

Instructor Effectiveness

1. Overall, the instructor was:

   1 - Poor   2 - Fair   3 - Good   4 - Very Good   5 - Excellent

Application After Training

1. What aspects of this workshop were most relevant to your work?

   _____

2. How will you use what you have learned when you return to the job?

   _____

Level 2: Learning Outcomes

What Is This Technique?

Level 2 evaluation is used to find out whether participants have acquired the knowledge, skills, and attitudes described by the course goals and objectives. It provides a measure of accomplishment that can be used for decisions regarding the success of the instructional approach and where improvements might be required.

The most common type of Level 2 tool is an achievement measure such as a test, role play, or exercise. However, in some areas of training, it is not feasible to use achievement measures due to the nature of the course goals, the style of the instructor-participant interactions, or other restrictions. In these cases, a self-report measure of learning can be used.

Level 2 measures complement Level 1 evaluations. Level 1 tells you whether people liked the course but not how much they learned, while Level 2 tells you how much they learned. The organization gains when positive results are achieved on both measures. Low scores on either evaluation can result in negative feedback to other potential participants.

When Is It Conducted?

End of course. Level 2 tools are usually given at the end of a course. However, in management and personal development courses, traditional Level 2 tools are often not used. In these cases, you can use self-report measures, open-ended questions, and activities such as role plays to obtain an estimate of participant accomplishment.

During the course. If it is a modular course, then a Level 2 tool is often used at the end of each module. This allows the instructor and the participants to know whether the objectives are being achieved as they progress through the course. It also removes some of the anxiety from having the total evaluation at the end.

Pretest. Level 2 measures are sometimes taken at the beginning of the course to find out whether learners already know the content. By comparing post-test scores to the pre-test scores, you can find out how much the participants learned in the course.

What Measures Are Available Using This Level?

It is important to know what the result or the outcome is when conducting diversity training. Change can be measured at the individual level in terms of knowledge, skill, or attitude improvement. Comparisons can be made across groups as well.

There are several levels of sophistication in training evaluation. As the degree of sophistication increases, the value tends to go up with it. A few examples of before and after measures, which quantify the results of a diversity training program, are as follows:

Diversity Knowledge Change

$$DKC \ = \ \frac{DK_A}{DK_B}$$

Where:

DKC = diversity knowledge change

DK_A = diversity knowledge level after training

DK_B = diversity knowledge level before training

This information can be obtained by pre- and post-testing. Scores can be obtained before and after each class or before and after the total program. This not only serves to demonstrate that people are learning what you want them to learn (*i.e.*, the objectives of the course), but points out specifically by test results what is not being learned. By reviewing the tests in class, you have an opportunity to reinforce the learning. Similar calculations can be used for skill and attitude changes.

Diversity Skill (Behavior) Change

$$DSC \ = \ \frac{DS_A}{DS_B}$$

Where:

DSC = observable change in diversity skills as a result of training

DS$_A$ = diversity skill demonstrated after training by work output, critical incidents of interpersonal relations, or other observable phenomena

DS$_B$ = diversity skill level existing previous to the training using the same criteria as above

Data for this diversity skill change ratio can be gathered through questionnaires, interviews, demonstrations, or observation with trainers, subordinates, peers, or supervisors. The key to obtaining something of value from any measure is in being specific in describing the diversity skills or behaviors to be evaluated. You can't put a value on vague explanations, but if you see someone doing something, you can measure and evaluate it.

Diversity Attitude Change

$$DAC = \frac{DA_A}{DA_B}$$

Where:

DAC = diversity attitude change

DAA = diversity attitude level after training

DAB = diversity attitude level before training

If the objective is to go beyond knowledge or skill change to attitude change, the same pre- and post-testing method can be used. In this case, either a standard or a specially designed and validated attitude instrument would be used. Since attitudes are particularly vulnerable to influences in the environment, thought should be given to the timing of the post-test. Attitudes immediately after the training may be affected once the participants reenter the work environment. The change may be either positive or negative, and in either case will confound the change attributed to the diversity training program. A test six months after the conclusion of training could tell how much change has been impacted by the environment.

If you find that the environment does not support the new diversity attitudes, it does not make sense to continue to train. Unless you do post-testing, you will never know what happened.

At a perceptual level, four tools can be used for evaluating what participants learned from the training. The first tool is short and uses rating scales. It is used to determine the learning potential of each participant going into the course, whether the specified objectives were covered in the course, and what the participants rate as their personal levels of learning. The participants' learning potential basically asks, did the participant know this material before taking the course, or was there room for improvement?

The accomplishment section asks how the participants perceive their personal accomplishment of that particular objective. This tool provides good statistical data on each participant's perception of accomplishment.

To score this self-assessment, record how many "0's" and "1's" there are under Learning Potential. Then record the total number of "0's" and "1's" under Covered in the Course. For the last column, find the total of the responses and divide by the number who actually answered it.

The second tool is a self-assessment that utilizes rating scales to compare before and after course learning. It asks for the participant's perceptions of their understanding of specific course objectives before and after taking a diversity training course. This tool allows you to see how much improvement there is, and to aggregate scores from a number of classes.

To score this self-assessment, subtract the "before" score from the "after" score. Add all of the remainders for a given item and divide by the total number of responses. Do this for each item.

The next tool is an open-ended questionnaire. Its purpose is to provide participant-generated answers to test their knowledge of the course material. This tool is better than the previous two tools for evaluating what the learner really knows and can recall, because it asks for actual knowledge instead of opinions. This tool takes more time to score than the first two, but it gives the evaluator a specific indication of whether the course objectives are being achieved.

To score this tool, prepare a short list of essential items of information that you are looking for in response to each item and decide how many points to give for each. Five or 10 points per item is a good choice. Depending on the number of questions, you can have a possible total of 50 or 100 points, and there is some latitude for giving partial credit for incomplete answers. Compare the participant's response to this key and give full or partial credit depending on how many key information items are included.

The last tool is a role-play behavioral checklist for diversity training and should be used in conjunction with appropriate role-play activities. The instructor or evaluator can use this tool to evaluate the performance of individuals or groups to determine whether they are exhibiting the appropriate attitudes or behaviors.

To use this tool, prepare for a role play in the normal manner. Once the role play begins, the participants should proceed through the entire scenario without prompting or feedback from the instructor. During the role play, the instructor looks for correct and incorrect examples of behavior related to the objectives in the checklist. For each item, the instructor indicates whether or not it was performed properly. After the scoring is finished, the instructor can then give feedback.

Figure 5-5

Self-Assessment of Learning
Diversity Self-Assessment

Instructions: For each course objective listed below, circle the number that represents your answer to each of the following questions:

Learning Potential

Was there anything new in this course for you to learn?

0 = I already knew this before the course started

1 = At the beginning of the course, I had room for improvement in this area

Covered in the Course

Was this objective actually taught in the course?

0 = This objective was not covered in the course

1 = This objective was covered in the course

Personal Learning Accomplishment

How well did I learn this objective?

Circle the number that best represents your degree of learning ranging from:

1 = For little or no change

5 = If you believe that you achieved a satisfactory level of mastery

Table 5-6

Course Objectives	Learning Potential	Covered in Course?	How Well I Learned This in the Course		
As a result of taking this course, I am able to:			Little or None	Improved My Skill	Achieved Mastery
1. Identify demographic trends that have a strong impact on quality of work life, and workers	0 1	0 1	1 2	3	4 5
2. Define stereotyping, racism, sexism	0 1	0 1	1 2	3	4 5
3. Recognize the primary dimensions of perceived differences in cultural groups	0 1	0 1	1 2	3	4 5
4. Identify situations and employee responses that typically result in intercultural conflicts	0 1	0 1	1 2	3	4 5

The following tool provides a "before" and "after" self-assessment of learning. You can subtract the first score from the second one to determine how much participants have changed.

Table 5-7

Learning Self-Assessment
Diversity Pre- and Post-Course Self-Assessment

Instructions: Circle the number that represents your choice.

Course Objectives	Before Taking the Class	After Taking the Class
As a result of taking this course, I am able to:	Before taking the diversity training course, my level of knowledge or competency for this objective was	After taking the diversity training course my level of knowledge or competency for this objective is
1. Recognize cultural stereotyping and biases toward race, gender, ethnicity, physical characteristic, and other differences	1 2 3 4 5 Low Moderate High	1 2 3 4 5 Low Moderate High
Understand my own cultural conditioning and how that may consciously or unconsciously influence my interactions with others	1 2 3 4 5 Low Moderate High	1 2 3 4 5 Low Moderate High

Figure 5-8

Figure 5-8

Knowledge of Diversity Issues
Assessment of Diversity-Related Knowledge

Instructions: For each question, write your answer in the space provided.

1. What are the advantages for using diversity training in the workplace?

_____

_____

2. What are the definitions of culture, ethnicity, prejudice, sexism, and racism?

_____

_____

3. What are your responsibilities in dealing with issues of diversity?

_____

_____

Figure 5-9

Learning Outcomes Role Play
Diversity Role Play Checklist

Group#_____ Group Members:_____

Instructor:_____ Course:_____

Instructions: For each skill, indicate whether or not it was demonstrated by the participant(s) by circling the appropriate number.

Skill	Demonstrated	Comments
1. Recognize and responded to instances of stereotyping and biased decision making within the work group.	0=NO 1=Yes	
2. Used strategies to counteract instances of bias in the work group	0=NO 1=Yes	
3. Informed others of unbiased and biased attitudes in a constructive manner	0=NO 1=Yes	
4. Displayed behaviors which are characteristic of effective and united teams	0=NO 1=Yes	

Level 3: Transfer of Training

What Is This Technique?

One of the primary goals of diversity training is to improve employee opportunity and performance on the job. The purpose of Level 3 evaluation is to find out whether course participants have transferred their newly-learned diversity knowledge, skills, and values to the job. This helps you determine how effective the course is, where to make improvements, how to further build workforce satisfaction, and improve productivity.

It is also useful, whenever possible, to find out why transfer has or has not occurred. Failure to transfer can be caused by things other than lack of learning. For example, successful transfer requires additional coaching and support on the job. If this does not happen, or if employees simply do not get the opportunity to use what they have learned, then you will not see transfer even though they may have learned the skills in your diversity course. In these cases, the course might be working just fine, and improvements are needed in the workplace to encourage and support transfer.

When Is It Used?

Level 3 evaluation takes place after the course is completed and participants have had enough time to demonstrate their attitudes and skills on the job. This can occur immediately after training, but usually takes longer for nontechnical skills such as diversity.

▶ **Immediate transfer.** When the learning outcomes are highly related to job performance, then transfer may occur almost immediately. Even if it does, it is important to determine whether the transfer continues to operate over a longer period of time or stops due to insufficient training or lack of support on the job.

▶ **One to three months after training.** Other kinds of training can require one to three months before evidence of transfer occurs. These include complex skills involving management and human interactions, or development skills that require time and practice to mature. Some of the diversity attitudes and skills could transfer rather quickly, but others would require a longer time. This is because it takes time to learn how to use the new attitudes and skills in the actual work environment, and situations that call for some of these skills might not occur frequently. The best time for Level 3 evaluation of diversity training is probably one to three months after the course.

What Measures Are Available Using This Level?

Participant Post-Training Surveys. This section contains tools that evaluate the effectiveness with which employees are taking new skills back to the job. The purpose of the format is to provide employees and their managers with similar evaluation tools, then compare the results to get the two perceptions. With parallel evaluation forms, it is easier to directly compare results from specific questions without loss of interpretation.

The first tool is the longest and most detailed in this section, and it parallels one of the other tools in the manager's post-training section. Here the participants are asked to circle the appropriate response regarding how well the course prepared them, how frequently they use the new attitude or skill, and how important it is to their job responsibilities. This tool will provide good statistical data, especially when paired with its management counterpart, and reveal perceptual similarities and differences between the employee and the manager.

Manager's Post-Training Evaluations. The tools in this section can be used as stand-alone measuring devices or in conjunction with their counterparts.

The second tool is a long stand-alone tool that combines the characteristics of the ranked and open-ended question type. This format provides numerical results for statistical analysis as well as verbal responses to add specificity.

The third tool parallels the first tool in the

participant post-training section. It is intended to provide a detailed method for comparing perceptions of the employee and the manager. Again, the viewpoint was changed to focus on the manager's observation of the employee. Besides the removal of the Prepared column, all other instructions are the same.

The last tool is a diversity checklist. This tool is designed to be used by managers to record whether they actually observed an employee using diversity attitudes and behaviors. Specific behavioral objectives that the employee should be applying to the job are listed on the left. Through observation, managers can record the date they observed that particular behavior, the level of satisfaction in performing the behavior, and their comments and suggestions. This tool is particularly helpful to track various employees' uses of the different skills learned in the diversity training course.

In some organizations, employee-manager contact is limited. If the employee's manager is not in a position to observe the employee on a regular basis, alternative methods and tools should be used. In some situations, this tool can be adapted to be used with other individuals who have regular contact with the employee, such as peers, subordinates, and customers.

Participant Tool

Figure 5-10

Applying Diversity Training On-the-Job: Participant Version

For each task listed below, please indicate how well the training course prepared you, how often you actually use it, and the importance of this skill to your job responsibilities.

Instructions: Circle the appropriate number in the column that represents your opinion.

Specific Task	Prepared	Use	Importance
	How well did the course prepare you to perform this task?	How often do you use this knowledge or skill on the job?	How important is this skill or knowledge to your job?
1. Create an inclusive work environment where individuals are treated fairly	0= Poorly 1= Somewhat 2= Very Well	0= Poorly 1= Somewhat 2= Very Well	0= Not At All 1= Somewhat 2= Very Much
2. Analyze diverse viewpoints to make planning decisions and solve work problems	0= Poorly 1= Somewhat 2= Very Well	0= Poorly 1= Somewhat 2= Very Well	0= Not At All 1= Somewhat 2= Very Much
3. Values and encourage open communication, input, opinions, and ideas from others	0= Poorly 1= Somewhat 2= Very Well	0= Poorly 1= Somewhat 2= Very Well	0= Not At All 1= Somewhat 2= Very Much
4. Model trust, openness, fairness, and respect for the individual in daily behavior	0= Poorly 1= Somewhat 2= Very Well	0= Poorly 1= Somewhat 2= Very Well	0= Not At All 1= Somewhat 2= Very Much

Manager's Tool

Figure 5-11

Manager's Post-Training Survey
Satisfaction with Diversity Training Course Effectiveness

Instructions: Circle the number that best reflects your opinion. Add comments whenever possible. This information will help us estimate the effectiveness of the diversity training and improve it.

For each of the following behaviors, please rate your satisfaction with your employee's performance:

1. Works effectively with people of different race, gender, and sexual orientation

1	2	3	4	5
Not Satisfied		Satisfied		Very Satisfied

2. Combats prejudice and discrimination

1	2	3	4	5
Not Satisfied		Satisfied		Very Satisfied

3. Responds sensitively to ideas or behaviors that differ form those of the dominant culture

1	2	3	4	5
Not Satisfied		Satisfied		Very Satisfied

4. Creates a climate in which everyone is respected and treated fairly regardless of race, age, gender, religion, disability, color, or sexual orientation

1	2	3	4	5
Not Satisfied		Satisfied		Very Satisfied

5. Overall, how satisfied are you that the Diversity Training Course provided skills and values that are relevant to the workplace?

1	2	3	4	5
Not Satisfied		Satisfied		Very Satisfied

Comments:_____

6. Overall, how satisfied are you with your employees' ability to apply skills and values that they learned in Diversity Training?

1	2	3	4	5
Not Satisfied		Satisfied		Very Satisfied

Comments:_____

Figure 5-12

Manager's Post-Training Survey
Applying Diversity Training On-the-Job: Manager's Version

For each task listed below, please indicate how often your
employees actually use these skills and how important they are to
his/her job responsibilities.

Instructions: Circle the number in each column that represents
your opinion.

Specific Task	Use	Importance
	How often does your employee use this skill?	**Is this skill important to his/her job responsibilities?**
1. Create an inclusive work environment where individuals are treated fairly	1=Almost Never 2=Seldom 3=Usually 4=Almost Always	0=No 1=Somewhat 2=Very Much
2. Analyze diverse viewpoints to make planning decisions and solve work problems	1=Almost Never 2=Seldom 3=Usually 4=Almost Always	0=No 1=Somewhat 2=Very Much
3. Values and encourage open communication, input, opinions, and ideas from others.	1=Almost Never 2=Seldom 3=Usually 4=Almost Always	0=No 1=Somewhat 2=Very Much
4. Model trust, openness, fairness, and respect for the individual in daily behavior	1=Almost Never 2=Seldom 3=Usually 4=Almost Always	0=No 1=Somewhat 2=Very Much

Figure 5-13

Diversity Behavior Checklist
Performance Checklist for Diversity Training Transfer

Reviewed Employee:_____ Diversity Course:_____

Reviewing Supervisor:_____ Current Date:_____

Period of Observation: Start:_____ Stop:_____

Instructions: Respond to the following items for each skill:

Dates Observed: *What day did you observe the employee perform the skill?* List the dates on which you observed the skill being performed. If you observed the skill more than once on a given day, repeat the date for each observation.

Performance Rating: *How well did s/he perform the skill?* If you observed the skill, circle the appropriate number in the second column that best represents your overall assessment of the employee's performance.

Comments: Please provide any additional information which you feel is important in the third column (*e.g.,* unusual circumstances, environmental factors, or details about the performance).

Skill to Be Reviewed	Dates	Performance Rating	Comments
1. Encourages pride, trust, and group identity		1=Needs Improvement 2 3=Satisfactory 4 5=Very Competent	
2. Treats people fairly and equitably		1=Needs Improvement 2 3=Satisfactory 4 5=Very Competent	

3. Values and capitalizes on team's diverse skills and backgrounds.		1=Needs Improvement 2 3=Satisfactory 4 5=Very Competent	

Performance Change

Another means of measuring level 3 transfer of training is to monitor changes in diverse work group performance appraisal ratings in relationship to receiving diversity training.

$$\text{PC} = \frac{P_A}{P_B}$$

Where:

PC = change in work performance as measured by the organization's performance appraisal system

PA = latest review score from a performance appraisal conducted at least 90 days after the diversity training

PB = performance review score from the performance appraisal conducted prior to the diversity training

Since performance appraisal scales are usually small (*e.g.*, 1 through 5 or 1 through 6), the difference in a single point may appear dramatic in terms of percentage change. Caution should be exercised in discussing an individual's performance change or you may be accused of overstatement. This measure takes on more meaning when a large number of appraisals are compared and consistently positive results appear.

A word of warning. There may be a halo effect. That is, the evaluator knows the employee went through training and expects improved performance. If the evaluator is not careful, something that is not there may be inferred.

Level 4: Organizational Results

What Is This Technique?

The ultimate purpose of training is to help the organization achieve its goals. This means that, in addition to transferring new skills/attitudes to the job, the results of training must have a positive effect on the organization. For example, let's assume that people show the desirable diversity behaviors at work. They are sensitive to their biases and overcome them by treating people as individuals. The next question is whether this results in desirable organizational performance that meets diversity objectives such as:

- ► Everyone feeling like they are part of the work team

- ► Fewer problems and grievances

- ► Higher productivity, morale, *etc.*

If training was the appropriate solution to this problem, or an important part of the solution, then we would expect to see these organizational benefits. This is the purpose of Level 4 evaluation.

Level 4 evaluation can occur at several levels. The first is the perceptual level. As with other levels of evaluation, it is possible to discover whether people perceive improvements in the expected areas of change. The second is performance, which is used to determine whether there are measurable improvements in organizational performance. The final level is financial. It uses processes for estimating whether there is a financial gain when the costs of training are compared to measurable benefits. These financial measures are the focus of Level 5: Return on Investment.

The focus of our examination of Level 4 measures will be concentrated at the perceptual level.

When Is It Used?

Like Level 3 evaluation, Level 4 is undertaken after the course has ended. Usually the time lapse is longer than for Level 3 evaluation. This is because organizational results occur sometime after the skills are actually transferred to the job. Typically the interval is three to six months after training, but in some cases it may be as long as nine to 12 months after training. (It can be sooner if there is reason to believe that changes could occur in less time.)

What Measures Are Available Using This Level?

Organizational Results Survey. This tool is used to

measure how much effect the training has had on the organizational environment and practice. This survey lists some possible organizational impacts the training can have, and provides a rating scale that asks if the evaluator (often the manager) agrees or does not agree that these impacts have occurred. This higher level evaluation will assist management in determining if the training has had the desired organizational impact. It is an effective way to gauge the perceptual return on training investment for the organization.

Figure 5-14

Organizational Results Survey
Organizational Impact Evaluation

Instructions: Rate each item by circling the number that represents your opinion.

Organizational Results	Rating		
	Strongly Disagree	Somewhat Agree	Strongly Agree
1. Diversity is part of the everyday communication at all employee levels.	1 2	3	4 5
2. Managers and employees are able to communicate about differences more freely.	1 2	3	4 5
3. The work climate for women, minorities, and other members of diverse groups has improved.	1 2	3	4 5
4. Women, minorities, and other members of diverse groups feel part of the work team.	1 2	3	4 5

5. The selection rates of qualified women, minorities, and other members of diverse groups for hiring and promotions has increased.	1	2	3	4	5
6. The diversity of the work force has increased.	1	2	3	4	5
7. Employees are taking personal responsibility for monitoring the work environment and responding to cases of discrimination and harassment.	1	2	3	4	5
8. Managers are taking personal responsibility for monitoring the work environment and responding to cases of discrimination and harassment.	1	2	3	4	5
9. The work environment does not tolerate racism, sexism, and insensitive behavior toward members of diverse groups.	1	2	3	4	5
10. After the training, there might have been an initial increase in discrimination complaints, but there was a decline over time.	1	2	3	4	5

Level 5: Return on Training Investment

What Is This Technique?

Possibly the ultimate level of evaluation is to compare the financial benefits of a program to the cost of that program. This comparison is the elusive goal of many diversity professionals.

First, you must have useful techniques to assign values to program data, particularly in those areas where it is fairly difficult. Data must be transformed into dollar values before the financial benefit can be calculated. This includes exploring calculations such as the value of increased output (*e.g.*, the average dollar sale, average profit per sale, etc), the value of cost savings (*e.g.*, actual savings in raw materials, supplies, time value of money), the value of time savings (*e.g.*, wages/salaries and benefits saved, reduced training time, penalty avoidance), the value of improved quality (*e.g.*, error reduction, increased accuracy, reduced waste, reduced rework, improved morale, reduced mistakes), and the value of "soft" data (*e.g.*, existing data/historical costs, expert opinion, participant estimation of values/costs, management estimation of values/costs).

Second, the methods of comparisons can be explored, the most common being return on investment (ROI). Using this procedure, Return on Training Investment can be calculated as well as other important measures.

When Is It Used?

Like Level 4 evaluation, Level 5 is undertaken after the course has ended. Usually the time lapse is the same as Level 4 or slightly longer to align with organizational data reporting periods.

The calculation of the return for a Diversity training program is not feasible or realistic in all cases. Even if the perceived benefits have been converted to dollar savings, the mere calculation of the return communicates to a perceptive manager more preciseness in the evaluation than may be there. Usually, the ROI calculation should be used when the program benefits can be clearly documented and substantiated, even if they are subjective. If management believes in the method of calculating the benefits, then they will have confidence in the value for the return. The nature of the program can also have a bearing on whether or not it makes sense to calculate a return. Management may believe, without question, an ROI calculation for sales training programs focused on diverse market penetration. They can easily see how an improvement can be documented and a value tied to it.

On the other hand, an ROI for a program that teaches managers the principles of transactional analysis for diversity may be difficult to swallow — even for the most understanding management staff. Therefore, the key considerations are reliability of the data and credibility of the conclusions based upon subjective data.

What Measures Are Available Using This Level?

The return on investment is an important calculation for diversity professionals. Yet, it is a figure that must be used with caution and care. There are many ways that it can be interpreted or misinterpreted. This section gives some general guidelines to help calculate a return, interpret its meaning, and calculate other costs and benefits.

Defining Return on Investment

Return on investment (ROI) may appear to be improper terminology for the diversity field. The expression originates in finance and accounting and usually refers to the pre-tax contribution measured against controllable assets. In formula form it is expressed as:

$$\text{Average ROI} = \frac{\text{pretax earnings}}{\text{average investment}}$$

It measures the anticipated profitability of an investment and is used as a standard measure of the performance of divisions or profit centers within a business.

The investment portion of the formula represents capital expenditures such as a training facility or equipment plus initial development or production costs. The original investment figure or production costs can be used. Also, the original investment figure can be used, or the present book value can be expressed as the average investment over a period of time. If the diversity program is a one-time offering, then the figure is the original investment.

However, if the initial costs are spread over a period of time, then the average book value is usually more appropriate. This value is essentially half the initial costs since, through depreciation, a certain fixed part of investment is written off each year over the life of the investment.

In many situations a group of employees are to be trained at one time, so the investment figure is the total cost of analysis, development, delivery, and evaluation lumped together for the bottom part of the equation. The benefits are then calculated assuming that all participants attend the program or have attended the program, depending on whether the return is a prediction or a reflection of what has happened.

To keep calculations simple, it is recommended that the return be based on pretax conditions. This avoids the issue of investment tax credits, depreciation, tax shields, and other related items.

To illustrate this calculation, assume that a work-life and family training program had initial costs of $50,000. The program will have a useful life of three years with negligible residual value at that time. During the three-year period, the program produces a net savings of $30,000, or $10,000 per year ($30,000/3). The average investment is $25,000 ($50,000/2) since the average book value is essentially half the costs. The average return is:

$$\text{Average ROI} = \frac{\text{annual savings}}{\text{average investment}}$$

$$= \frac{\$10,000}{\$25,000}$$

$$= \mathbf{40\%}$$

Return on investment is sometimes used loosely to represent the return on assets (ROA) or the return on equity (ROE). Equity usually refers to the net worth of an organization. The assets represent the total assets employed to generate earnings, including debt. The ROA and ROE are terms that are more meaningful when evaluating the entire organization or a division. ROI is usually sufficient for evaluating expenditures relating to a diversity program.

Finance and accounting personnel may take issue with calculations involving the return on investment for efforts such as a diversity program. Nevertheless, the expression is fairly common and conveys an adequate meaning of financial evaluation.

Some professionals suggest a more appropriate name is return on training. Others avoid the word "return" and would simply calculate the dollar savings as a result of the program, which is basically the benefits minus costs. These figures may be more meaningful to managers to keep from getting the ROI calculation confused with similar calculations for capital expenditures.

ROI may be calculated prior to a diversity program to estimate the potential cost effectiveness or after a program has been conducted to measure the results achieved. The methods of calculation are the same. However, the estimated return before a program is usually calculated for a proposal to implement the program. The data for its calculation are more subjective and usually less reliable than the data after the program is completed. Because of this factor, management may require a higher ROI for a diversity program in the proposal stage.

Measurement by the Numbers Is Required

If you want to measure the effects and value of training at any level, you can. You can even put a dollar value on the impact. The approaches discussed here are proof that no matter what type of diversity training has been applied, it can be measured and evaluated. The most important requirement is that you follow the principles and steps described in this section.

If it were easy to measure diversity training effects, many more people would be doing this as a matter of routine. However, there is distance still to be traveled and much to be learned. When we start to show management exactly how much value diversity training programs can contribute to the process of building an inclusive work environment, the programs will become a strategic requirement.

References

Hubbard, Edward E., *How to Calculate Diversity Return on Investment*. California: Global Insights Publishing, 1999.

Hubbard, Edward E., *The Diversity Scorecard: Evaluating the Impact of Diversity on Organizational Performance*. Massachusetts: Butterworth-Heinemann, Elsevier Publishing, 2004.

Hubbard, Edward E., *The Diversity Discipline: Implementing Diversity Work with a Strategy, Structure, and ROI Measurement Focus*. California: Global Insights Publishing, 2009.

Jackson, Susan E., *Diversity in the Workplace*. New York: The Guilford Press, 1992.

Plummer, Deborah L., *Handbook of Diversity Management*. Maryland: University Press of America, Inc. 2003

CHAPTER 6

Calculating the ROI Value of Training

Introduction

Taking the time to calculate the costs and benefits of a diversity training initiative is an essential step in developing the Diversity Return on Investment calculation since costs represents the denominator in the DROI® formula. It is equally critical to pay attention to both the costs and benefits of any diversity initiative that you put in place. In practice, however, the costs are often more easily captured than benefits. This chapter of the book highlights some specific methods for accumulating and calculating costs, outlining the specific costs that should be captured, identifying benefits as well as identifying the steps to perform a DROI® calculation to highlight the value and worth of Diversity Training.

Strategies for Accumulating and Calculating Costs

Importance of Costs

Capturing costs is challenging because the figures must be accurate, reliable and realistic. Although most organizations develop costs with a lot less difficulty than developing the economic value of the benefits, calculating the true cost and benefits of diversity can be difficult. And of course, this affects the Diversity Return on Investment. On the cost side, the total diversity organization budget is usually a number that is easily developed, however, determining the specific costs of a diversity training initiative, including related indirect costs, and its benefits can be far more elusive. To develop a realistic DROI®, costs must be accurate and credible. Otherwise, the painstaking difficulty and attention to benefits will be wasted because of inadequate or inaccurate costs.

Today there is more pressure than ever before to report all initiative costs or what is commonly referred to as fully loaded costs. This takes the cost profile beyond the direct cost of diversity initiatives and includes the time all participants are involved in developing and participating in the diversity training initiative, including all costs, benefits, and other overhead. Taking the conservative approach to calculate diversity return on investment, you should plan to report fully loaded costs. With this approach, all costs that can be identified and linked to a particular diversity training initiative are included. The philosophy is simple: When in doubt in the denominator, put it in (*i.e.*, if it is questionable whether a cost should be included, the rule suggests that it should be included, even if the organizational costs guidelines don't require it). When diversity ROI is reported to your target audiences, it should withstand even the closest scrutiny in terms of its accuracy and credibility. The only way to meet this test is to ensure that all costs are included.

The Impact of Reporting Costs Without Benefits

It is dangerous to communicate the costs of diversity training initiatives without presenting the corresponding benefits. Unfortunately, many organizations have fallen into this trap. Because costs can be easily collected, they are presented to management in all types of ingenious ways such as cost of the initiative, cost per diversity hire, and cost per diversity training hour and the like. While these may be helpful for efficiency comparisons, it may present a real problem if they are presented without the benefit side of the story. When executives review Diversity Training initiative costs, a logical question comes to mind: What benefit was received for this investment in diversity training? This can be a typical management reaction, particularly when costs are perceived to be very high. Some organizations have adopted a policy of not communicating diversity initiatives costs data unless the benefits can be captured and presented along with the costs. Even if the benefit data are subjective and intangible, they are included with the cost data. This helps keep balance when diversity efforts are viewed by others.

Typical Cost Categories

One of the most important tasks you must complete is to define which specific costs are included in the tabulation of costs in a diversity initiative. This task involves decisions that will be made by the diversity staff and usually approved by management. If appropriate, the finance and accounting staff may need to approve the list. The following table shows the recommended cost categories for a fully loaded, conservative approach to estimating costs. Each category is described in the paragraphs that follow.

Table 6-1

Diversity Initiative Cost Categories		
Cost Item	Prorated	Expensed
Needs Assessment	X	
Design and Development	X	
Acquisition	X	
Delivery Internal		X
▶ Salaries/Benefits-Facilitators/ Diversity Council Members		X
▶ Materials and Fees		
▶ Travel/Lodging/Meals		X
▶ Facilities		X
▶ Salaries/Benefits-Participants		X
▶ Contact Time		X
▶ Travel Time		X
▶ Preparation Time		X
Evaluation	X	
Overhead/Diversity Department	X	

Prorated vs. Direct Costs

Usually all costs related to a diversity training initiative or project are captured and expensed to that initiative or project. However, three categories are usually prorated over several sessions of the same project or initiative. Needs assessment, design and development, and acquisition are all significant costs that should be prorated over a basic shelf life of the diversity initiative. With a conservative approach, the shelf life of a diversity initiative should be very short. Some organizations consider one year of operation, others may consider two or three years. If there is some question about the specific time period to be used in the proration formula, the finance and accounting staff should be consulted.

A brief example will illustrate the proration for development costs. In a large industrial organization, a diversity training initiative was created to improve multicultural teamwork and innovation at a cost of $98,000. The diversity initiative's development team anticipated that the project would have a three-year life cycle before it would have to be updated. The revision costs at the end of the three years were estimated to be about one-half of the original development costs, or $49,000. The diversity project would be conducted with 25 groups in a three-year period, with a DROI® calculation planned for one specific group. Since the project would have one-half of its residual value at the end of three years, one-half of the cost should be written off for this three-year period. Thus, the $49,000, representing half of the development costs, would be spread over the 25 groups as a prorated development cost. Therefore, a DROI® for one group would have a development cost of approximately $2,000 ($49,000/25 = $1,960) included in the cost profile.

Benefits Factor

When presenting participant and diversity staff salaries associated with diversity initiatives, the benefits factor should be included. This number is usually well known in the organization and is used in other costing formulas. It represents the cost of all employee benefits expressed as a percent of base salaries. In some organizations, this value is as high as 50%-60%. In others, it may be as low as 25%-30%. The average in the USA is 38%.

Needs Assessment

One of the most often overlooked items is the cost of conducting a needs assessment in the exploratory phase of a diversity training intervention. In some diversity initiatives, this cost is zero because the diversity initiative is conducted without a needs assessment (such as mandatory diversity awareness training in some organizations). However, as more organizations focus increased attention on identifying a validated need for a Diversity Training or other initiatives, this item will become a more significant cost in the future. All costs associated with the needs assessment should be captured to the fullest extent possible. These costs include the time of staff members conducting the assessment, direct fees and expenses for external consultants who conduct the needs assessment, and internal services and supplies used in the analysis. The total costs are usually prorated over the life of the diversity initiative or project. Depending on the type and nature of the diversity initiative, the shelf life should be kept to a very reasonable number in the one- to two-year timeframe. Of course the exception would be very expensive initiatives (such as building a daycare facility and its operation) which are not expected to change significantly for several years.

Design and Development Costs

One of the more significant items is the cost of designing and developing the Diversity Training initiative. These costs include internal staff time in both design and development and the purchase of supplies, equipment, materials, audio-visual media, and other items directly related to the Diversity Training initiative. It would also include the use of consultants. As with the needs assessment costs, design and development costs are usually prorated, perhaps using the same timeframe. One or two years is recommended unless the initiative is not expected to change for many years and the costs are very significant.

Acquisition Costs

In lieu of development costs, many organizations will purchase some diversity programs to use directly or in a modified format. This is often the case with diversity training materials. The acquisition costs for these programs include the purchase price for the instructional materials, train-the-trainer sessions, licensing agreements, and other costs associated with the right to deliver the program. These acquisition costs should be prorated using the same rationale outlined for design and development costs; one to two years should be sufficient. If modification of the program is needed or some additional development is required, these costs should be included as development costs. In practice, many diversity-training programs have both acquisition costs and development costs.

Delivery Costs

Usually the largest segment of the Diversity Training initiative costs would be those associated with delivering the initiative. Five major categories are included.

Salaries of Facilitators/Diversity Council Members. The salaries of facilitators or diversity council members should be included. If a facilitator or council member is involved in more than one program, the time should be allocated to the specific program under review. If external facilitators are used, all charges should be included for the session. The important issue is to capture all of the direct time of internal employees or external consultants who work directly with the diversity initiative. The benefits factor should be included each time direct labor cost are involved. This factor is a widely accepted value, usually generated by the finance and accounting staff. It is usually in the range of 30%-40%.

Diversity Project Materials and Fees. Specific diversity initiative materials such as notebooks, textbooks, case studies, exercises, speakers on key topics, and participant workbooks should be included in the delivery costs, along with license fees, user fees, and royalty payments. Pens, paper, certificates, and calculators are also included in this category.

Travel, Lodging, and Meals. Direct travel for participants, facilitators, diversity council members, or others is included. Lodging and meals are included for participants during travel, as well as meals during the stay if they are participating in education or training-based diversity initiatives. Refreshments should also be included.

Facilities. The direct cost of any purchased facilities should be included. For external programs, this is the direct charge from conference centers, hotels, or motels. If the diversity initiative is implemented and an in-house facility is used that represents a cost to the organization, the cost should be estimated and included, even if it is not the practice to include facilities' costs in other reports.

Participants' Salaries and Benefits. The salaries plus employee benefits of participants represent an expense that should be included. For situations where the diversity initiative has already taken place, these costs can be estimated using average or midpoint values for salaries in typical job classifications. When a program is targeted for a DROI® calculation, participants can provide their actual salaries directly and in a confidential manner.

Evaluation

Usually the total evaluation costs is included in the diversity initiative's costs to compute the fully loaded cost. DROI® costs include the cost of developing the evaluation strategy, designing instruments, collecting data, data analysis, and report preparation and distribution. Cost categories include time, materials, purchased instruments, or surveys. A case can be made to prorate the evaluation costs over several programs instead of charging the total amount as an expense. For example, if 25 sessions of a training-based diversity initiative are conducted in a three-year period and one group is selected for a DROI® study, then the DROI® costs could logically be prorated over the 25 sessions. Since the results of the DROI® analysis should reflect the success of the other programs as will perhaps result in changes that will influence the other programs as well.

Overhead

A final charge is the cost of overhead, the additional costs in the diversity function not directly related to a particular diversity initiative. The overhead category represents and diversity department cost not considered in the above calculations. Typical items include the cost of clerical support, the departmental office expenses, salaries of the diversity department staff members (this is prorated if diversity is not your full-time job responsibility, e.g., you have other functions attached to your job such as EEO, Organizational Effectiveness, etc.), and other fixed costs. Some organizations obtain an estimate for allocation by dividing the total overhead by the number of diversity initiative days for the year (examining how many days you spent or will spend involved in an actual diversity initiative for the year). This becomes a standard value to use in calculations.

Costs are important and should be fully loaded in the DROI® calculation. From a practical standpoint, including some of the costs may be optional, based upon the organization's guidelines and philosophy. However, because of the scrutiny involved in DROI® calculations, it is recommended that all costs are included, even if it goes beyond the requirements of the company policy.

Cost and Consequences of
Not Implementing A Diversity Initiative

For some organizations, the consequences of not implementing a diversity initiative can be very serious. An organization's inability to perform adequately due to real or perceived barriers caused by a poor diversity inclusive climate might mean that it is unable to take on additional business or that it may lose existing business because of a dysfunctional workforce, poor connections with ethnic markets, high turnover, *etc.* Also, diversity can help an organization avoid serious operational problems (accidents) or non-compliance problems, *etc.* Measuring the consequences of not implementing a diversity initiative is noteworthy and involves the following steps:

▶ Establish that there is a potential problem, loss, or opportunity.

▶ Isolate the problems that lack of performance may create such as non-compliance issues, loss of business, or the inability to take on additional business.

▶ Develop an estimate of the potential value of the problem, loss or opportunity.

▶ If other factors are involved, determine the impact of each factor on the loss of income.

▶ Estimate the total cost of the diversity initiative using the techniques described in this book.

▶ Compare the benefits with costs.

This approach has also some disadvantages. The potential loss of income can be highly subjective and difficult to measure. Also, it may be difficult to isolate the factors involved and to determine their weight relative to lost income. Because of these concerns, this approach to evaluating the diversity return on investment is limited to certain types of initiatives, programs, or situations.

Defining Return on Investment

The term "return on Investment (ROI) in diversity is often misunderstood and misused. In some situations, a very broad definition for ROI includes any benefit from the program. In these situations, ROI is a vague concept in which even subjective data linked to the diversity effort is included in the concept of the return. As stated earlier, the expression originates in finance and accounting and usually refers to the pre-tax contribution measured against controllable assets. In formula form it is expressed as:

$$\text{Average ROI} = \frac{\text{pretax earnings}}{\text{average investment}}$$

It measures the anticipated profitability of an investment and is used as a standard measure of the performance of divisions or profit centers within a business.

The investment portion of the formula represents capital expenditures such as a training facility for the diversity awareness program or equipment plus initial development or production costs. The original investment figure or production costs can be used. Also, the original investment figure can be used, or the present book value can be expressed as the average investment over a period of time. If the diversity program is a one-time offering, then the figure is the original investment.

However, if the initial costs are spread over a period of time, then the average book value is usually more appropriate. This value is essentially half the initial costs since, through depreciation, a certain fixed part of investment is written off each year over the life of the investment.

In many situations, a group of employees are to be trained in diversity at one time, so the investment figure is the total cost of analysis, development, delivery, and evaluation lumped together for the bottom part of the equation. The benefits are then calculated assuming that all participants attend the program or have attended the program, depending on whether the return is a prediction or a reflection of what has happened.

To keep calculations simple, it is recommended that the return be based on pretax conditions. This avoids the issue of investment tax credits, depreciation, tax shields, and other related items.

Sound complicated? It can be, depending on the particular accounting methodology you subscribe to. For the purposes of calculating diversity's return on investment in the "live laboratory of organizations, we will use an effective, simple, straightforward accounting approach.

In this book, Diversity Return on Investment (DROI®) is more precise and is meant to represent an actual value developed by comparing the diversity initiative costs to benefits. The two most common measures are the cost/benefit ratio and the (DROI®) formula. Both are presented here along with other approaches that calculate a return.

For some time now, diversity practitioners and researchers have tried to calculate the actual return on investment in diversity. If diversity is considered an investment—not an expense—then it is appropriate to place the diversity investment in the same funding process as other investments, such as the investment in equipment and facilities. Although these other investments are quite different, management often views them in the same way. Thus, it is critical to the success of the diversity field to develop specific values that reflect Diversity's Return on Investment (DROI®).

To illustrate this calculation, assume that a work-life and family training program had initial costs of $50,000. The program will have a useful life of three years with negligible residual value at that time. During the three-year period, the program produces a net savings of $30,000, or $10,000 per year ($30,000/3). The average investment is $25,000 ($50,000/2) since the average book value is essentially half the costs. The average return is:

$$\text{Average ROI} = \frac{\text{annual savings}}{\text{average investment}}$$

$$= \frac{\$10,000}{\$25,000}$$

$$= 40\%$$

ROI may be calculated prior to a diversity program to estimate the potential cost effectiveness or after a program has been conducted to measure the results achieved. The methods of calculation are the same. However, the estimated return before a program is usually calculated for a proposal to implement the program. The data for its calculation are more subjective and usually less reliable than the data after the program is completed. Because of this factor, management may require a higher ROI for a diversity program in the proposal stage.

DROI® Fundamentals

Annualized Values

All of the DROI® formulas presented here will use annualized values so that the first year impact of the diversity initiative's investment is developed. Using annualized values is becoming a generally accepted "best practice" for developing DROI® in organizations. This approach is a conservative way to develop DROI®, since many short-term diversity initiatives have added value in the second or third year. For long-term diversity initiatives, annualized values are inappropriate and longer time frames need to be used.

When selecting the approach to measure DROI®, it is important to communicate to the target audience the formula used and the assumptions made to arrive at the decision to use it. This action can avoid misunderstandings and confusion surrounding how the DROI® value was actually developed. Although several approaches are described in this chapter, two stand out as the preferred methods—the benefit/cost ratio and the basic DROI® formula.

These two approaches are described next, along with brief coverage of the other approaches.

Benefit/Cost Ratio

One of the earliest methods for evaluating investments in diversity initiatives is the benefit/costs ratio (read as the benefits-to-costs ratio). This method compares the benefits of the program to the costs in a ratio. In formula form, the ratio is:

$$\text{BCR} = \frac{\text{Diversity Initiative Benefits}}{\text{Diversity Initiative Costs}}$$

In simple terms, the BCR compares the annual economic benefits of the diversity initiative to the cost of the initiative. A BCR of one means that the benefits equal the costs. A BCR of two, usually written as 2:1, indicates that for each dollar spent on the diversity initiative, two dollars were returned as benefits.

The following example will illustrate the use of the benefit/cost ratio. A diversity leadership initiative, designed for managers and supervisors, was implemented at an electric and gas utility. In a follow-up evaluation, action planning and business performance monitoring were used to capture benefits. The first year payoff for the initiative was $1,077,750. The total fully loaded implementation cost was $215,500. Thus, the ratio was:

$$\text{BCR} = \frac{\$1,077,750}{\$215,500} = 5:1$$

For every one dollar invested in the diversity initiative, five dollars in benefits were returned.

The principal advantage of using this approach is that it avoids traditional financial measures so that there is no confusion when comparing diversity initiative investments with other investments in the organization. Investments in plants, equipment, or subsidiaries, for example, are not usually evaluated with the benefits/cost method. Some executives prefer not to use the same method to compare the returns in diversity with the returns on other investments. Consequently, this method for calculating diversity return on investment stands out as a unique type of evaluation.

Unfortunately, there is no standard as to what constitutes an acceptable benefits/cost ratio for diversity. A standard should be established within an organization, perhaps even for a specific type of diversity initiative. However, a 1:1 ratio is unacceptable for most programs, and in some organizations, a 1.25:1 ratio is required, where 1.25 times the cost is the benefit.

The DROI® Formula

Perhaps the most appropriate formula for evaluating an investment in a diversity initiative is the net initiative benefits divided by costs. The ratio is usually expressed as a percent where the fractional values are multiplied by 100. In formula form, the DROI formula is expressed as:

$$\text{DROI}^® \ (\%) \ = \ \frac{\text{Net Diversity Initiative Benefits}}{\text{Diversity Initiative Costs}} \ \times \ 100$$

Net benefits are diversity initiative benefits minus the diversity initiative costs. The DROI® value is related to the BCR by a factor of one. For example, a BCR of 2.45 is the same as a DROI® value of 145%. This formula is essentially the same as ROI in other types of investments. For example, when a firm builds a new plant, the ROI is found by dividing annual earnings by the investment. The annual earnings is comparable to net benefits (annual benefits minus the cost). The investment is comparable to the diversity initiative costs, which represent the investment in the initiative.

A DROI® on a diversity investment of 50% means that the costs are recovered and an additional 50% of the costs are reported as "earnings." A diversity investment of 150% indicates that the costs have been recovered and an additional 1.5 multiplied by the costs is captured as "earnings." An example illustrates the DROI® calculation. Magnavox Electronics Systems Company conducted an 18-week literacy program for entry level electrical and mechanical assemblers (Ford, D, "Three R's in the Workplace," in *In Action: Measuring Return on Investment*, Vol.1, J. Phillips (Ed.), Alexandria, VA: American Society for Training and Development, 1994, pp85-104.) The results of the program were impressive. Productivity and quality alone yielded an annual value of $321,600. The total fully loaded costs for the program were $38,233. Thus, the diversity return on investment becomes:

$$\text{DROI}® \; (\%) \; = \; \frac{\$321,600 - \$38,233}{\$38,233} \; \text{X} \; 100 \; = \; 741\%$$

For each dollar invested, Magnavox received $7.4 dollars in return after the cost of the program had been recovered.

Using the DROI® formula essentially places diversity investments on a level playing field with other investments using the same formula and similar concepts. Key management and financial executives who regularly use ROI with other investments easily understand the DROI® calculation.

While there are no generally accepted standards, some organizations establish a minimum requirement or hurdle rate for an ROI in human resource-based programs such as training. An ROI minimum of 25% is set by some organizations. The same will eventually come true for diversity initiatives. This target value in training is usually above the percentage required for other types of investments. The rationale: the ROI process for training is still relatively new and often involves some subjective input, including estimations. Because of that, a higher standard is required or suggested, with 25% being the desired figure for these organizations. I feel it is mandatory that DROI® calculations follow suit.

Other ROI Methods

In addition to the traditional DROI® formula previously described, several other measures may be used under the general term of return on investment. These measures are designed primarily for evaluating other types of financial measures, but may offer some alternate possibilities in measuring the return on investments in diversity.

Payback Period

The payback period is a common method for evaluating capital expenditures. With this approach, the annual cash proceeds (savings) produced by an investment are equated to the original cash outlay required by the investment to arrive at some multiple of cash proceeds equal to the original investment. Measurement is usually in terms of years and months. For example, if the cost savings generated from a diversity initiative are constant each year, the payback period is determined by dividing the total original cash investment (development costs, outside program purchases, *etc.*) by the amount of the expected annual or actual savings. The savings represent the net savings after the diversity initiative's expenses are subtracted. To illustrate this calculation, assume that an initial diversity initiative cost is $100,000 with a three-year useful life. The annual net savings from the diversity initiative are expected to be $40,000. Thus, the payback period becomes:

Payback Period = Total Investment /Annual Savings

Payback Period = $100,000/$40,000 = 2.5 Years

The diversity initiative will contribute a "payback" of the original investment in 2.5 years.

The payback period is simple to use, but has the limitation of ignoring the time value of money. It has not enjoyed widespread use in evaluating investments such as training or human resources in general.

Calculating DROI® Using A Worth and Value Approach

When Diversity training has worked, it provides something of value to the organization. Diversity training begins as a response to a need or opportunity in an organization. Establishing the value brings training full circle to the needs, problems, or opportunities it was originally intended to serve. The specific purpose of establishing value is to determine what value has been returned to the organization by diversity training and whether, considering the costs of training, that value was worth the expense. Because many organizations find it difficult to quantify the gains, comparing training gains with training costs can be challenging.

A key question for the Diversity practitioner to answer is "What is the organization getting for the money invested?" Every enterprise, whether for profit or not, is faced with deciding how to allocate limited resources to achieve its goals. Internally, competition for funds can be as fierce as in the external marketplace. When times are tough and money and resources are limited, decision makers must make economically sound budgeting choices. When faced with multiple requests for budgets, they require, for each case, a clear answer to the question: "What will the organization get for its money?" Another way of asking this question is: "What will the ROI be?" (Stolovitch and Keeps, 2004).

Currently, very few Diversity Training Practitioners can answer these questions readily and with confidence. The result of not being able to demonstrate worth and DROI® for Diversity training programs (DTROI®) has extremely negative consequences. When the crunch comes, this places the Diversity training initiatives at a disadvantage. Showing activity (for example, how many people were/will be trained; how many courses were/will be developed) only provides decision makers with cost information. Where is the benefit? What is the return to the organization in concrete, comprehensible terms?

At this point, you should have completed a full Diversity Training Needs Analysis based upon your stakeholder's or client's request and wish to demonstrate *potential* worth and DTROI® for the diversity training intervention. In worth analysis, you estimate your benefit-to-cost ratios. In DTROI® calculations, conducted once a training project is implemented, you no longer have to estimate. You work with real figures unless you wish to show potential ROI beforehand. The following process works for both. For "worth," you estimate the value of deficiencies or improvements, frequencies of occurrences, and amount of impact. For the calculation of true

DROI®, you use real figures. Both cases apply the same calculation patterns. Worth analysis requires you to calculate the worth (W) of a set of proposed Diversity learning or performance interventions by comparing the anticipated value (V) against the estimated costs (C). The formula is as follows:

$$W = V/C$$

The result is a ratio. For example, if the value of what you expect to achieve from your Diversity Training interventions is $500,000 and the cost $100,000, then worth is as follows:

$$W = V/C$$
$$= 500,000/100,000$$
$$= 5:1$$

This is your worth or benefit-to-cost ratio. DROI® calculations result in a percentage. If you wish to know your Diversity "return" (DROI®), you must subtract your costs (C) from your value (V) and then divide by your cost (C) and multiply by 100 as follows:

$$ROI = (V - C)/C \ X \ 100$$

The result is a percentage. For example, if you obtain $500,000 in value from expenditures of $100,000, you calculate ROI as follows:

$$DROI® = (V - C)/C \ X \ 100$$
$$= (500,000 - 100,000)/100,000 \ X \ 100$$
$$= 400 \text{ percent}$$

Although DROI® uses real figures following intervention implementation, you can also calculate potential DROI®, just like worth, by estimating future costs and value.

Key Considerations for your Level 4 Organizational Results Analysis and Calculating Diversity Training ROI (DTROI®)

After you have measured the changes in on-the-job performance and have calculated the cost of providing Diversity training, you are ready to begin conducting a Level 4, Organizational Results evaluation. This involves calculating the DROI® value of Diversity training.

Many organizations find it difficult to quantify the gains. In addition, the numbers alone do not tell the whole story (Fisher and Ruffino, 1996). For example, an organization decided that management training was needed in order to reduce the number of grievances filed by employees. A training program was designed and implemented. A Level 3 evaluation was conducted and the following data were collected:

▶ **Pre-training and Post-training Measures:** The grievance rates of the managers who attended training were compared for the six months before training and the six months after training. An analysis of these data found a significant difference in the pre-training and post-training grievance rates. However, the total decrease in grievances was small.

▶ **Comparison Measures:** A randomly selected comparison group was established. Managers in this group did not attend the training. The grievance rates of the managers who attended training were compared with the grievance rates of those who did not attend the training during the same six-month period. An analysis of these data found that the trained managers had significantly fewer grievances. The cost of the training was then calculated to be $500,000. The evaluator determined that handling grievances cost the agency $25,000 per grievance. The total number of grievances decreased by 15 during the six months following training. The cost savings from the training ($375,000) were less than the cost of designing and implementing the training. The evaluator summarized the results and recommended that the training be suspended because it failed to recover the full cost.

The evaluator in this example may have overlooked several factors, including:

▶ **Payback Time Period:** The evaluator failed to project the continued benefits of training beyond the six months studied. In determining the value of training, it is important to consider future "payoffs."

▶ **Other Benefits:** The evaluator failed to consider other benefits that may have been derived from the training. Decreased grievances may have resulted in improved morale or even increased productivity. In the example, comparison of the trained and the untrained managers could have revealed differences in employee morale or productivity. Often, evaluators sell their training short by measuring the benefits that are easiest to quantify (*e.g.,* number of grievances) or by failing to measure "spin-off" benefits.

▶ **Cost of Not Intervening:** There may be future costs if the problem continues. The evaluator may need to consider the cost to the organization if grievances keep increasing. Some problems tend to get worse over time.

▶ **Nonmonetary Payoffs:** It may be wrong to assume that the organization's only value is the bottom line. Decision makers may be willing to make a $125,000 investment in enhancing the skills of their managers. Decision makers may feel that this investment will pay off in nonmonetary ways (Fisher and Ruffino, 1996).

Most organizations are in the business of providing products and services to the public. Measuring the bottom line or cost savings from training may not take into account the positive impact of this training on the organization's employees and/or its reputation in the community and/or on its mission. Although it is important to operate an efficient organization, improved employee satisfaction alone may not always demonstrate the best return being generated.

When Is the Value of Training Established?

A Level 4 evaluation requires that you analyze the value of training before and after the training.

> ▶ **Before training, determine the anticipated value.**
> During the needs analysis process, you should work with decision makers to clarify the expected benefits and the amount of resources they are willing to invest to obtain these benefits. You may also want to identify the anticipated costs of not solving the problems being addressed by training.

> ▶ **After training, compare the anticipated value with the actual value.** After training, a comparison is made between the anticipated value and the actual value from training. At this point you should review the organization's original needs and determine if they have been met by training. If the needs have been met, you can then determine if the costs were as anticipated.

The anticipated benefits and costs should be identified before training. If this step is not completed during the training needs analysis, then you will need to work with decision makers to attach a value to your comparison of benefits and costs. In the previous example, a finding that it cost $125,000 to decrease grievances by a total of 15 during a six-month period has no meaning until the organization places a value on that result. Decision makers may feel that decreasing grievances is worth the investment of $125,000 because the trained managers will model skills that will be passed along to "future generations" of managers. (Fisher and Ruffino, 1996).

How Is the Value of Training Established?

As we saw in the example discussed above, in general, the following steps can be used to calculate the DTROI® value of Diversity training:

- ▶ Identify the organizational benefits

- ▶ Establish the worth

- ▶ Compare the benefits to the costs

- ▶ Determine the value

- ▶ Report the results

Let's explore each step in a little more detail.

Identify the Organizational Benefits

After you have determined that on-the-job performance has changed as a result of training, you can then ask the question: **"How did the organization benefit from changes in on-the-job performance?"**

This step translates the changes in on-the-job performance into the following types of organizational benefits:

- ▶ **Increased Output:** Changes in output are the goal of many training programs. In most situations, the value of increased output can be calculated easily.

- ▶ **Time Savings:** Many training programs are aimed at reducing the time it takes for participants to perform particular job functions or tasks. Time savings are important because employee time is money.

▶ **Improved Quality:** Training is also developed to improve the quality of performance.

▶ **Error Avoidance:** In some cases, training may be provided to maintain the current levels of performance and to avoid potential errors.

At this stage in the evaluation process, you should review the potential organizational benefits identified during the training needs analysis. If your training needs analysis did not identify potential organizational benefits, then you should now identify the types of benefits you think may have resulted from the change in on-the-job performance. You may want to select more than one type of benefit. For example, you may want to look at both increases in outputs and improvements in quality.

Establish the Worth

The next step is to establish the worth of the benefits. To do this, you should:

▶ Measure the benefit using the selected indicators (error reduction, improved quality, increased productivity, *etc.*). If you selected number of errors and customer complaints as your indicators, you should now figure the difference between the pre-training and the post-training levels of these indicators.

▶ Convert the benefit change into a dollar value indicating

its worth. Next, you should convert the change in benefits into a dollar amount. If this step is not completed, you may find it impossible to compare costs and benefits. By not converting the benefit to a dollar value, you would be comparing "apples to oranges." Therefore, if you cannot establish an objective cost figure for the benefits, you should use a subjective value.

Some common types of indicators are summarized below.

Table 6-2

Organizational Benefits	Indicators
Increased Outputs	· Number of products produced or services provided · Number of processes completed · Amount of backlogged work
Time Savings	· Amount of nonproductive time · Amount of sick leave and/or tardiness · Amount of overtime · Amount of break-in time for new employees
Improved Quality	· Amount of positive versus negative feedback from diverse customers · Amount of positive versus negative results of external audits and inspections (EEOC, External Diversity Advisory Board Audits, *etc.*) · Amount of rework required · Number of innovative solutions or products developed · Amount of employee involvement in decision making · Changes in employee morale/motivation · Frequency of communication within the organization · Number of grievances and other personnel problems

Error Reduction	• Number of errors
	• Number of safety-related complaints from employees and customers
	• Number of safety problems
	• Number of accidents
	• Number of rule/procedure violations

Source: Adapted from Fisher and Ruffino, 1996

Some benefits are easy to convert into dollar amounts. For example, if there was a reduction in the amount of overtime spent during a comparable time period, you can simply subtract the amount of overtime spent before training from the amount of overtime spent after training. However, some benefits are more difficult to convert to dollar amounts. The following sample methods can be used to determine the dollar value of some training benefits. For other types of training benefits, you may need to develop your own method for converting the benefits into dollars. These sample methods can be used to help you develop your own strategies for approaching this task. For the purposes of this discussion to establish worth, we will focus on two examples: 1) the steps to convert improved quality and 2) the steps to convert increased output.

Establishing the Worth of Increased Output

The following method establishes a measure of the worth resulting from an increase in outputs. This method should be used only if the outputs have no established market value. For example: If your outputs were widgets and they sold for $30, you could simply multiply the value of the widgets ($30) by the total increased number of widgets (200) to yield a value of $6,000. However, because your some of your diversity-related outputs may not have a market value, you may need to establish the worth based on the employee's salary and increased productivity. This method provides a way of valuing increased outputs when the outputs have no market worth.

Table 6-3

Establishing the Worth of Increased Output		
Step	Calculation	Example
1. Determine the employee's annual compensation (salary plus benefits).		$30,000
2. Determine the average number of outputs per person per year BEFORE training.		1,000
3. Determine the average number of outputs per person per year AFTER training.		1,200
4. Determine the total difference in outputs.	AFTER training outputs (line 3) minus BEFORE training outputs (line 2)	200
5. Calculate the percentage of change in outputs.	Total difference in outputs (line 4) divided by BEFORE training outputs (line 2)	20%
6. Establish the worth of the change.	Annual compensation (line 1) times Percentage of change (line 5)	$6,000

Source: Adapted from Fisher and Ruffino, 1996

Establishing the Worth of Improved Quality

The following method establishes a subjective measure of the worth resulting from improved quality such as in improved workforce climate and culture. This method assumes that the organization does not get full value unless personnel are performing at a high-quality level. In addition, the assessment of quality is based on a subjective, 1-to-10 rating. You should use this method only when you cannot determine a more objective measure of improved quality.

In this example, let's assume that the organization has determined that having a "high quality workplace" that is fair and employees are respected is critical to business performance and its mission. They have estimated that having the diversity skills and cultural competencies to effectively "communicate across differences" is at the very least 20% of the job performed by employees. In fact, employees are trained to perform a "seven-step competency model" process to communicate across differences if they find themselves in a difficult or conflict interaction with another employee. Based upon this background, we could calculate the value and worth of the Diversity Training intervention as shown below.

Table 6-4

Establishing the Worth of Improved Quality		
Step	**Calculation**	**Example**
1. Determine the employee's annual compensation (salary plus benefits).		$50,000
2. Determine percentage of job being trained.		20%
3. Multiply annual compensation by percentage of job being trained.	Annual compensation (line 1) Times % of job being trained (line 2)	$10,000
4. On a 1-to-10 scale, rate performance quality level BEFORE training.	1 = Low Quality 5 = Moderate Quality 10 = High Quality	3
5. Multiply the BEFORE rating by 10 to determine the quality percentage.	Quality rating (line 4) times 10	30%
6. Multiply the dollars spent on that portion of the job by the quality.	Dollars spent on portion of job (line 3) times Quality percentage (line 5)	$3,000
7. On a 1-to-10 scale, rate quality level AFTER training.	1 = Low Quality 5 = Moderate Quality 10 = High Quality	8
8. Multiply the AFTER quality rating by 10 to determine the new quality percentage.	Quality rating (line 7) times 10	80 %
9. Multiply the dollars spent on that portion of the job by the quality percentage.	Dollars spent on portion of job (line 3) times Quality percentage (line 8)	$8,000
10. Determine the difference between BEFORE and AFTER worth.	Value of AFTER (line 9) minus Value of BEFORE (line 6)	$5,000

Source: Adapted from Fisher and Ruffino, 1996

Compare the Benefits to the Costs

The next step is to compare the worth of the benefits to the costs of providing Diversity training. You can make this comparison by: *(Example)*

$$\begin{array}{lr}
\text{[Benefits per person} = \$7{,}000] & \\
- \text{ [Cost of training per person } \$3{,}000] & \\
\hline
= \quad \text{Return per person} \quad = \quad \$4{,}000 &
\end{array}$$

Times number of people trained = [4,000 X 100] = Total Return-on-Investment: $400,000

Calculating the Return-on-Investment Ratio

As long as costs stay constant, the return-on-investment ratio can be used to project future benefits of conducting the same training. For example, if the return-on-investment ratio is 3:1 and the organization invests $100,000 in training, then you can project that the benefits from conducting this training in the future would be $300,000. To calculate the return-on-investment ratio, use the following formula:

$$\frac{\text{[Benefits per person} = \$7{,}000]}{\text{[Cost of training per person } \$3{,}000]}$$

Benefit-Cost Ratio: 2.3:1 (sometimes called Return-on-Investment Ratio)

$$\begin{array}{l}
\text{DROI\%} = [\$7{,}000] - [\$3{,}000] = \$4{,}000 \\
\qquad\qquad [\, / \ \$3{,}000] = 1.33 \\
\qquad\qquad [\text{X } 100] = 133\%
\end{array}$$

Depending on how you established the worth of your benefits, your return-on-investment amounts or ratios may show only the savings accrued during the first year. You may want to project the continued benefits to be derived from the training over time before calculating your return-on-investment ratio.

Determine the Value

It is great to get a return-on-investment from a training effort. However, not all training will result in a return-on-investment. And, even if the training saved $100,000, it is important to link how those savings enhanced the organization's ability to achieve its mission. Therefore, this step involves placing a value on the return derived from the training.

Establishing the value of training is not as simple as comparing costs and benefits after the training. It is important to clarify organizational expectations both before and after the training. For example: If Diversity training improved the language literacy, cultural competency, and interpretation skills of hospital personnel thus increasing the emergency room response time of hospital personnel, more lives may be saved. How much is that Diversity training worth to the organization?

This step is easy if organizational goals were established with decision makers during the needs analysis phase. An organizational goal for a Diversity training effort should state:

**What the organization will gain as
a result of the Diversity training**

and

**The amount the organization is
willing to invest to obtain that gain.**

When organizational goals have been established, completing
this step is just a matter of determining whether the goals were
accomplished. If organizational goals do not exist, then you may
want to interview decision makers or convene a focus group to
help you determine the value derived from the training.

Report the Results

Once you have an understanding of how the return from the
Diversity training efforts supports the organization's mission,
then you can develop your evaluation report. The following list
highlights some items you may want to include in your evaluation
report. You may want to use the following guidance when
developing your evaluation report.

Guidelines for Reporting Results

▶ Describe the methods used to collect information.

▶ Describe the rationale for how dollar amounts were
estimated or derived .

▶ Include any limitations of the data collected (*e.g.*, survey-
response rate).

▶ Use tables, graphs, and figures to present results.

▶ Support each recommendation by summarizing related
data.

▶ Provide an executive summary with references to where additional data can be found.

▶ Check the accuracy of the data presented and make sure there are no editorial mistakes.

▶ Make sure there are no big surprises. Keep decision makers involved and informed throughout the evaluation

Table 6-5

Evaluation Report Outline

I. Overall Findings and Recommendations
    A. Organizational Goals
    B. Training Conducted
    C. Major Findings
        1. Goals Accomplished
        2. Return-on-Investment
        3. Other Benefits Derived
        4. Summary of On-the-Job Performance Changes
    D. Recommendations
        1. Suggested Modifications to Training
        2. Need for Additional Evaluation

II. Evaluation Methods
    A. Purpose of the Evaluation
    B. Evaluation Methods
    C. Limitations of the Evaluation Findings

III. Measures of On-the-Job Performance
    A. Types of Data Collected
    B. Data Sources and Sampling Techniques
    C. Data Collection Methods
    D. Results
        1. Data Summary
        2. Interpretation of Findings
    E. Limitations of Findings

IV. Cost of Training
    A. Cost Items Included
    B. Rationale for How Costs Were Determined
    C. Results

V. Return-on-Investment
    A. Type of Benefits Measured
    B. How Worth Was Established
    C. Results

Appendixes
    Appendix 1: Copies of Data Collection Instruments
    Appendix 2: List of Individuals Interviewed/Documents Reviewed
    Appendix 3: Statistical Reports

Source: Adapted from Fisher and Ruffino, 1996

Establishing the value of training can be a very challenging undertaking. If you do not have the resources needed to conduct a comprehensive Diversity return-on-investment study, you may find it helpful to collect information from decision makers on the perceived benefits derived from the Diversity training program (Fisher and Ruffino, 1996).

Reporting Your Results Should Not Be An Afterthought

Reporting your diversity measurement results is critical to the total evaluation process. It should not be left as an afterthought simply because you are achieving the intended results. These results have to be communicated in a conservative tone and effective manner to demonstrate and maintain diversity's link to the business bottom-line. Your goal must be to communicate diversity results in facts, figures and financials that make the business case for performance.

DROI® Issues to Consider

DROI® Complexity

Developing the return on investment from diversity is a complex issue. This book was designed to take the complex process of diversity measurement and diversity return on investment concepts and simplify them by breaking them down into small steps so it is understandable, practical and acceptable to a variety of audiences.

Cautions When Using DROI®

Because of the complexity and sensitivity of the DROI® process, caution is needed when developing, calculating, and communicating the return on investment. The implementation of the DROI® process is a very important issue, and is a goal of many diversity organizations. Addressing the following issues can help make certain the process does not go off track.

The DROI® process should be developed for an initiative where a serious needs assessment has been conducted. Because of the evaluation problems that can develop when it is not clear that a need exists, it is recommended that the DROI® study be conducted with initiatives that have had a comprehensive needs assessment. However, I am well aware that in some cases practical considerations and management requests may prohibit this suggested requirement.

The DROI® analysis should always include one or more strategies for isolating the effects of the diversity initiative. Because of the importance of accounting for the influences of other factors, this step in the process must not be ignored. Too often, an excellent study—from what appears to be a very successful diversity effort—is perceived to be worthless because there was no attempt to account for other factors. Omission of this step seriously diminishes the credibility of the diversity initiative study.

When making estimates, use the most reliable and credible sources. Because estimates are critical to any type of analysis, they will usually be an important part of a DROI® study. When they are used, they should be developed properly and obtained from the most reliable and credible sources—those individuals who best understand the overall situation and can provide accurate estimates.

Take a conservative approach when developing both benefits and costs. Conservatism in DROI® analysis builds accuracy and credibility. What matters most is how the target audience perceives the value of the data. A conservative approach is always recommended for both the numerator of the DROI® formula (diversity initiative benefits) and the denominator (diversity initiative costs).

Use caution when comparing the ROI in diversity with other financial returns. There are many ways to calculate the return on funds invested or assets employed. The ROI is just one of them. Although the calculation for DROI® uses the same basic formula as in other investment evaluations, it may not be fully understood by the target group. Its calculation method and its meaning should be clearly communicated. More importantly, it should be an item accepted by management as an appropriate measure for measuring diversity results. This kind of credibility must be earned by taking the time to complete all of the assessment and measurement steps in the process.

Involve management in developing the return. Management ultimately makes the decision if a DROI® value is acceptable. To the extent possible, management should be involved in setting parameters for calculations and establishing targets by which diversity initiatives are considered acceptable within the organization.

Approach sensitive and controversial issues with caution.
Occasionally, sensitive and controversial issues will be generated
when discussing a DROI® value. It is best to avoid debates over
what is measurable and what is not measurable unless there is
clear evidence of the issue in question. The issue can be included
in the overall measurement process as an intangible benefit. Also,
some initiatives are so fundamental to the organization's survival
that any attempt to measure them is unnecessary. For example,
a diversity initiative designed to improve customer service in
a customer-focused organization may escape the scrutiny of a
DROI® evaluation, on the assumption that if the initiative is well
designed, it will improve customer service. As more organizations
implement DROI® studies and standards evolve, the diversity
measurement discipline will have increasing evidence that DROI®
values can be trusted with accuracy and validity.

Develop case studies of your DROI® calculations. Creating
case studies of your DROI® studies can help educate your
organization on the full value of your efforts and the benefits
in measuring diversity results. These successes and learning
opportunities can help other diversity initiatives and other diversity
personnel throughout the organization. Hubbard & Hubbard, Inc.
offers specific workshops designed to help you develop or turn
your existing data into a diversity business case study as well as
train Diversity Practitioners and others in the detailed approaches
to calculate DROI®, methods to isolate diversity's contribution from
others, methods to convert Diversity's contribution to money, and
many other ROI-driven processes.

Do not boast about a high return. It is not unusual to generate what appears to be a very high DTROI® for a diversity Training initiative. This can open the diversity organization up to undue criticism and scrutiny even when the numbers are an accurate reflection of the facts. The value for DTROI® will be built as more members of the organization come to understand the processes through their own participation on diversity initiative teams and obvious improvements in organizational climate and performance.

Do not try to use DROI® on every diversity initiative.
Some diversity initiatives are difficult to quantify, and a DROI® calculation may not be feasible. Other methods of presenting the benefits may be more appropriate. It is helpful to set specific criteria for the selection of diversity initiatives that will be evaluated when using the DROI® level of analyses.

Identifying and Incorporating Intangible Measures

Not all measures can or should be converted to monetary values. By design, some are captured and reported as intangible measures. Although they may not be perceived as valuable as the measures converted to monetary values, intangible measures are critical to the overall evaluation process. In some diversity initiatives such as diversity leadership training, managing multicultural conflict, *etc.*, the intangible, or non-monetary benefits can be more important than monetary or tangible measures. Consequently, these measures should be monitored and reported as part of the overall evaluation. In practice, every diversity initiative, regardless of its nature, scope, and content, will have intangible measures associated with it. The challenge is to efficiently identify and report them. Some of the more typical variables that are referred to as "intangible" include the following:

Table 6-6

Typical Intangible Variables Linked with Diversity	
▶ Attitude Survey Data	▶ Employee Transfers
▶ Organizational Commitment	▶ Customer Satisfaction Survey Data
▶ Climate Survey Data	▶ Customer Complaints
▶ Employee Complaints	▶ Customer Response Time
▶ Grievances	▶ Teamwork
▶ Discrimination Complaints	▶ Cooperation
▶ Stress Reduction	▶ Conflict
▶ Employee Turnover	▶ Decisiveness
▶ Employee Absenteeism	▶ Communication
▶ Employee Tardiness	▶ *Etc.*

The good news is that with the advent of processes such as causal pathway analysis, and staple measurement processes such as correlation, linear and multiple regression, and even cross-tab correlation, we are pinpointing diversity contributions in many of the so-called "intangible" areas and converting diversity initiative contributions into monetary values. Nonetheless, if you need to report these variables as intangibles, then the following procedures will help.

Identification of Measures

Intangible measures can be identified in several ways representing different time frames. First, they can be uncovered early in the process, during the needs assessment. Once identified, the tangible data are planned for collection as part of the overall data collection strategy. For example, a multicultural marketing training for team leaders program has several hard data measures linked to the effort. An intangible measure, employee satisfaction, is identified and monitored with no plans to convert it to a monetary value. Thus, from the beginning, this measure is destined to be a non-monetary benefit reported along with the DROI results.

A second way in which an intangible benefit is identified is to discuss with the sponsors or management what is the impact of the diversity training initiative as he or she sees it. They can usually identify intangible measures that are expected to be influenced by the diversity initiative.

The third way in which an intangible measure is identified is during an attempt to convert the data to monetary values. If the process used to convert the data to monetary value loses credibility, the measure should be reported as an intangible benefit. For example, in a multicultural selling skills program, customer satisfaction is identified early in the initiative as one of the measures of the diversity initiative's success. A conversion to monetary values was attempted. However, the process of assigning a value to the data lost credibility; therefore, customer satisfaction was reported as an intangible. Currently, to remedy this problem, correlation's can be made linking customer satisfaction to customer retention and then customer retention to dollars to calculate the benefits in hard dollar amounts.

The fourth way in which an intangible measure is identified is during a follow-up evaluation. Although the measure was neither expected nor anticipated in the initial diversity initiative design, the measure surfaces on a questionnaire, in an interview, or during a focus group. Questions are often asked about other improvements linked to the diversity initiative. Several intangible measures are usually provided and there are no planned attempts to place a value on the actual measure. For example, in a diverse customer service training initiative, participants were asked specifically what had improved about their work area and their relationship with their multicultural customer base as a result of the application of the skills they acquired in the diversity training initiative. The participants provided over a dozen intangible measures, which managers perceived to be linked directly with the diversity training initiative.

DTROI® is a Critical Link For Success

Calculating Diversity Training Return On Investment (DTROI®) is a critical link for success in diversity management and organizational performance in the future. "You can't manage what you don't measure" and managing and leveraging diversity is fast becoming a business imperative. If diversity training initiatives are not approached in a systematic, logical, and planned way, DTROI® will not be possible and consequently, diversity will not become integrated into the fabric of the organization. In order to be seen as credible and on par with other business disciplines, it is imperative that "diversity science" is added to our current processes built on theory. At Hubbard & Hubbard. Inc., we have dedicated ourselves to creating and building the "Diversity Sciences and Technologies to help forge Diversity and Inclusion as a professional discipline that is rooted in measurable organizational performance practices, impact and results!

I feel it is our job as diversity professionals to make certain that the credibility of diversity efforts do not suffer. We must build a strong business practice reputation using effective diversity analytic and measurement techniques such that diversity is seen as a key driver of organizational performance and success!

References

Hubbard, Edward E., *How to Calculate Diversity Return on Investment.*
California: Global Insights Publishing, 1999.

Hubbard, Edward E., *The Diversity Scorecard: Evaluating the Impact of Diversity on Organizational Performance.* Massachusetts: Butterworth-Heinemann, Elsevier Publishing, 2004.

Hubbard, Edward E., *The Diversity Discipline: Implementing Diversity Work with a Strategy, Structure, and ROI Measurement Focus.* California: Global Insights Publishing, 2009.

Jackson, Susan E., *Diversity in the Workplace.* New York: The Guilford Press, 1992.

Plummer, Deborah L., *Handbook of Diversity Management.* Maryland: University Press of America, Inc. 2003

Stolovitch, Harold D., & Keeps, Erica J., *Front-End Analysis and Return on Investment Toolkit.* John Wiley & Sons, Inc., 2004

Fisher, Sharon G., & Ruffino, Barbara J., *Establishing the Value of Training.* HRD Publishing, Massachusetts, 1996.

CHAPTER 7

The Hubbard Five Level Diversity Measurement Taxonomy

Introduction

As stated previously, Diversity measurement is one of several activities that must be undertaken to achieve an organization's strategic business objectives. The only way to determine if a diversity intervention is having the desired effect is to use analysis, evaluation and a formal diversity measurement taxonomy which helps to categorize the level of measurement sophistication and analyze the impact of the approach being utilized. The results of these activities can confirm the level of impact of a Diversity training initiative and identify the range of growth and improvements that are possible. Implementing a diversity training measurement strategy for evaluation can contribute to maximizing the organization's return on training investment (DTROI®).

The reason I developed this five-level diversity measurement taxonomy was to clarify the operating performance levels of a diversity training or other intervention and to further define the meaning of "diversity levels of evaluation." Some organizations only support diversity practitioner's work at a "compliance" level concerned primarily with meeting EEO and Affirmative Action requirements. Others operate at a much higher "strategic" level using applications demonstrating an advanced level of commitment and characterized by the integration and measurement of diversity initiatives for their strategic impact on identified business needs. However, they are both connected along a continuum that offers degrees of value at each level up to and including return on investment.

As a Diversity Training professional, it is critical to understand how training evaluation and analysis is aligned with these levels and the metrics and analytical indices used to measure your Diversity training performance must be consistent with each level's focus. For example, some Diversity training interventions will only be concerned with meeting a "compliance" standard whereas others may be developed to drive results and ROI.

These five levels are important and should be understood by diversity practitioners and professionals in the field who want to effectively measure the ROI of their Diversity Training initiatives. The Hubbard diversity five-level taxonomy represents a specific classification framework and process to evaluate a diversity intervention or aspects of the diversity change process. As you move from one level to the next, the process becomes more difficult and time intensive, yet provides more valuable information. None of the levels should be by-passed since each level is a part of the "chain of impact" that supports the "causal" link that the Diversity training can be classified as part of a larger strategy to drive ROI. In addition, these levels provide a glimpse into the strategic, holistic nature of the intervention. These levels include the following:

- ► Level 1: **Activities Focused Level or Intangibles**

- ► Level 2: Compliance

- ► Level 3: Inclusion

- ► Level 4: Strategic Performance

- ► Level 5: Profit-Focused ROI Level and Mission Focused ROI Level

Figure: 7-1

Hubbard Diversity Analytics and Metrics Taxonomy™	
Level	**Description**
Level 1: Activities Focused Level (Intangibles)	Diversity metric applications that highlight positive results that either cannot be converted to monetary values or would involve too much time or expense in the conversion to be worth the effort. The range of intangible outcomes is practically limitless. It is important to note that, even though any of the intangible benefits may not be converted in one evaluation study, they may be converted in another study or in another organization. Not all measures can or should be converted to monetary values. By design, some should be captured and reported as intangible measures. Although they may not be perceived as valuable as the measures converted to monetary values, as stated earlier, intangible measures are critical to the overall evaluation process.
Level 2: Compliance	Diversity metric applications "demonstrating a weak to moderate commitment to increasing minority representation within the organization." It presupposes cursory attention to diversity in compliance with EEO and Affirmative Action laws or concern with "representation level" mixtures of diverse people in the organization. Compliance level metrics foster a focus on diversity measurement to help assess the impact of the organization's diverse workforce recruiting and retention efforts. However, they tend to be limited to assuring the organization has met its Affirmative Action and/or EEO requirements. Organizations operating at this level are often only interested in whether diversity in the workforce is present in denominations that equal the Civilian Labor Force (CLF) or other representational benchmarks. Diversity metrics at this level are not often used to drive business or mission performance.

Hubbard Diversity Analytics and Metrics Taxonomy™	
Level	**Description**
Level 3: Inclusion	Diversity metric applications involving a higher level of commitment to diversity activities, accompanied by the strong support of senior management and the development of programs designed to build a diversity-friendly environment. It also includes building a diversity focused infrastructure to take advantage its diverse talent and capability. It is also important that the definition of diversity at this stage and its associated metrics are broad and inclusive, capturing all employee segments – gender, race, ethnicity, religion, sexual orientation, disability, *etc*. This helps move the diversity process from a "basic" stage to an "improved capability" stage that promotes full utilization of all people.
Level 4: Strategic Performance	Diversity metric applications demonstrating an advanced level of commitment and characterized by the integration and measurement of diversity initiatives for their strategic impact on identified business needs. It also includes the strategic use of formal scorecards, dashboards, and diversity focused bonus and incentive plans to create measurable change in the organization's performance. This helps move the diversity process from a "proactive" stage to building "strategic capability"

Hubbard Diversity Analytics and Metrics Taxonomy™	
Level	**Description**
Level 5: Diversity Return on Investment (DROI)	Diversity metric applications measuring the anticipated profitability of a diversity initiative investment. It is used as a means to measure the performance of an organization's application of diversity in financial terms.
	The investment portion of the formula represents capital expenditures such as a training facilities or equipment plus initial development or production costs. The original investment figure can be used or production costs, or the present book value can be expressed as the average investment over a period of time. If the diversity program is a one-time offering, then the figure is the original investment.
	However, if the initial costs are spread over a period of time, then the average book value is usually more appropriate. This value is essentially half the initial costs since, through depreciation, a certain fixed part of investment is written off each year over the life of the investment.

Note! The last four levels of evaluation build in sequence. That is, in order to assess that your organization's diversity measurement processes are operating at the next highest level, your metrics must include all of the metric levels below it. For example, if you feel your diversity metrics operate at the Strategic performance level, the organization must fully utilize metrics at the Compliance and Inclusion levels.

Let's take a closer look at each of these levels in more detail.

Activity-Level or Intangibles

Most successful diversity initiatives result in some intangible benefits. Activity or intangible (anecdotal) benefits should be measured and reported since they are often the first level of movement towards an objective. They can be used as additional evidence of a diversity initiative's success and can be presented as supportive qualitative data. Activity or intangibles may not carry the weight of measures that are expressed in dollars and cents, but they are still a very important part of the overall evaluation, and many executives are interested in these measures.

Activity or intangibles are defined as positive results that either cannot be converted to monetary values or would involve too much time or expense in the conversion to be worth the effort. They can include capturing the "effects" of Diversity training such as an employee's remarks "I don't know what you did to my manager in that training program, but he or she is now asking me for my opinion on things and getting me involved in decisions that affect me … wow, thanks" The range of intangible outcomes are practically limitless. It is important to note that, even though many of the intangible benefits may not be converted in one evaluation study, they may be converted in another study or in another organization. Not all measures can or should be converted to monetary values. By design, some should be captured and reported as intangible measures. Although they may not be perceived as valuable as the measures converted to monetary values, as stated earlier, intangible or activity-based measures can be important to the overall evaluation and change process.

In some diversity initiatives such as diversity leadership training, managing multicultural conflict, intangible effects on teamwork, job satisfaction, communication, and customer satisfaction, *etc.*, the intangible or non-monetary benefits can be more important than monetary or tangible measures. Consequently, these measures should be monitored and reported as part of the overall evaluation. In practice, every diversity initiative, regardless of its nature, scope, and content, will have activity-based or intangible measures associated with it. The challenge is to efficiently identify and report them.

A sample of diversity metrics or outcomes impacted at this level includes:

▶ Soft or qualitative measures or outcomes that cannot be quantified but are important outcomes for the organization.

Table 7-2

Typical Intangible Variables Linked with Diversity	
Attitude Survey Data	Employee Transfers
Organizational Commitment	Customer Satisfaction Survey Data
Climate Survey Data	Customer Complaints
Employee Complaints	Customer Response Time
Grievances	Teamwork
Discrimination Complaints	Cooperation
Stress Reduction	Conflict
Employee Turnover	Decisiveness
Employee Absenteeism	Communication
Employee Tardiness	*Etc.*

Compliance Level Diversity Metrics

At bare minimum, organizations must track diversity compliance regarding basic issues of workforce representation, costs of voluntary and involuntary turnover, and financial and other impacts of litigation.

The "Compliance" level diversity metrics are defined as those "demonstrating a weak to moderate commitment to increasing minority representation within the organization." It presupposes cursory attention to diversity in compliance with EEO and Affirmative Action laws or concern with "representation level" mixtures of diverse people in the organization. Compliance level metrics foster a focus on diversity measurement to help assess the impact of the organization's diverse workforce recruiting and retention efforts.

At the compliance level, the commitment to diversity focuses primarily on meeting a representation standard of diversity and avoiding doing things that fail to comply with the law.

A sample of diversity metrics impacted by training, at this level includes:

▶ Recruitment, Representation, Voluntary and Involuntary Turnover, and Litigation Exposure Reduction.

Inclusion Level Diversity Metrics

In order to advance your Diversity training efforts beyond the Compliance level to the third phase, the Inclusion level, it is necessary to focus your diversity training and measurement analysis at a deeper level that addresses key result areas such as reasonable accommodation, knowledge development, promotion, employee satisfaction, level of senior management commitment, *etc.* This helps move your diversity process from a "maintenance" stage to a "proactive" program.

Compliance level metrics helped lay the basic foundation. Inclusion level metrics help you take an in-depth look at your diversity process change strategy, then advance the process towards building a diversity infrastructure, systems, and an organizational capability.

Inclusion level metrics reflect a higher level of commitment to diversity interventions, accompanied by the strong support of senior management and the development of programs designed to build a diversity-friendly environment. It also includes building a diversity focused infrastructure to take advantage its diverse talent and capability.

In order to build your diversity efforts towards the "Inclusion Level" metrics performance, it is necessary to focus your diversity training and measurement efforts at an even deeper level that addresses key result areas such as fully represented candidate pools at all levels for promotion and succession planning, diversity-friendly policies, minority and women placements, minority staff who meet competence standards for placement in key assignments, minority and women individual development plans (IDPs) achieved by position and level. It is also important that the definition of diversity and associated metrics be broad and inclusive, capturing all employee segments — gender, race, ethnicity, religion, sexual orientation, disability, *etc.* This helps move the diversity process from a "proactive" stage to an "improved capability" stage that promotes full utilization of all people. It includes a broader but limited use of formal scorecards, dashboards, and diversity focused bonus and incentive plans that support inclusion based metrics.

Inclusion level training and metrics foster a wider spread utilization of diversity measurement to help assess and change the impact of diverse workforce promotion, employee satisfaction, and building commitment throughout the organization. Inclusion Level metrics help you integrate diversity into the organization's way of operating and utilizing diverse workforce talent and processes as a strategic resource for meeting goals and objectives.

A sample of diversity metrics impacted by training, at this level includes:

▶ Talent Pipeline Development, Retention, Environment and Culture Improvement, Knowledge Development, Work-life Improvement, Succession Planning, Promotion, Employee Satisfaction, Reasonable Accommodation, Leadership Accountability and Commitment, Diversity Initiatives Achievement, Supplier Diversity, and External Recognition, Human Capital Depletion, Compensation Equity, Employee Network Impact, Utilization Rates, *etc.*

Strategic Performance Level Diversity Metrics

In order to advance your Diversity training and measurement efforts beyond the Inclusion level to the fourth phase, the Strategic Performance level, it is necessary to focus diversity training and measurement analytics at a level that addresses whether or not your Diversity training initiatives have had a strategic impact on the organization's business strategy and/or its objectives. In general, examples include reducing or eliminating problems and/or increasing or taking advantage of opportunities.

The *Strategic Performance* level is defined as demonstrating an advanced level of commitment and characterized by the integration and measurement of diversity training initiatives for their strategic impact on identified business needs. It also includes the strategic use of scorecards, dashboards, and diversity focused bonus and incentive plans. This helps move the diversity process from a "proactive" stage to utilizing "strategic capability." It includes the full use of formal scorecards and diversity focused bonus and incentive plans that tie bonus percentage increases and payouts to Strategic Performance metric outcomes and DROI returns.

A sample of diversity metrics impacted by training, at this level includes:

▶ Productivity Improvement, Innovation, Creativity, Cycle-time Reduction, Market Share Improvement, Customer Retention and Satisfaction, Human Capital Readiness Level, Human Capital Competence Level, Human Capital Commitment Level, Human Capital Satisfaction Level, Climate Impact, and Cost Level, *etc.*

Diversity Return on Investment (DROI®) Level Diversity Metrics

Possibly the ultimate level of evaluation is to compare the financial benefits of a Diversity training program or initiative to the cost of that initiative. This comparison is the elusive goal of many diversity professionals. In order to advance your diversity efforts beyond the Strategic Performance level to the fifth phase, the Diversity ROI level, it is necessary to focus Diversity training and measurement analytics on the financial impact of the Diversity training initiative.

First, you must have effective techniques to assign values to diversity training initiative data, particularly in those areas where it is fairly difficult. Data must be transformed into dollar values before the financial benefit can be calculated. This includes exploring calculations such as the value of increased output (*e.g.*, the average dollar sale, average profit per sale, *etc.*), the value of cost savings (*e.g.*, actual savings in raw materials, supplies, time value of money), the value of time savings (*e.g.*, wages/salaries and benefits saved, reduced training time, penalty avoidance), the value of improved quality (*e.g.*, error reduction, increased accuracy, reduced waste, reduced rework, improved morale, reduced mistakes), and the value of "soft" data (*e.g.*, existing data/historical costs, expert opinion, participant estimation of values/costs, management estimation of values/costs).

Second, the methods of comparisons can be explored, the most common being return on investment (ROI). Using this procedure, Diversity Return on Investment (DROI®) can be calculated.

Diversity Return on Investment (DROI®) Level Definition

In formula form it is expressed as:

$$\text{Average ROI} = \frac{\text{pretax earnings}}{\text{average investment}}$$

The *Diversity Return on Investment* level is defined as measuring the anticipated profitability of a diversity initiative investment and its payback period. It is used as a means to measure the performance of an organization's application of diversity in financial terms.

The investment portion of the formula represents capital expenditures such as a training facilities or equipment plus initial development or production costs. The original investment figure can be used or production costs, or the present book value can be expressed as the average investment over a period of time. If the diversity program is a one-time offering, then the figure is the original investment.

However, if the initial costs are spread over a period of time, then the average book value is usually more appropriate. This value is essentially half the initial costs since, through depreciation, a certain fixed part of investment is written off each year over the life of the investment.

For example, in situations where a group of employees are to be trained at one time, the investment figure will be the total cost of analysis, development, delivery, and evaluation lumped together for the bottom part of the equation. The benefits are then calculated assuming that all participants attend the program or have attended the program, depending on whether the return is a prediction or a reflection of what has happened.

To keep calculations simple, it is recommended that the return be based on pretax conditions. This avoids the issue of investment tax credits, depreciation, tax shields, and other related items.

A sample of diversity metrics impacted by training at this level includes:

> ▶ **DROI® Level (ROI management of metrics):**
> DROI®, BCR, and Payback Period

Evaluating the DROI® Level provides the greatest challenge to diversity practitioners and professionals. After all, many times our primary objective is to show demonstrated, tangible results from our diversity training efforts that is more than the investment costs. However, evaluating DROI® and utilizing the Hubbard Diversity Analytics and Measurement Taxonomy™ (shown in below) is not only possible, it is a routine, structured process of certified diversity professionals trained by the HDM&P Institute.

The Diversity Measurement Performance taxonomy includes the following focus areas:

Table 7-3

The Hubbard Five Level Diversity Analytics and Measurement Taxonomy™
By Dr. Edward E. Hubbard, Copyright © 2005, All Rights Reserved

Rating Level	Profit Focused Description	Government / Non-Profit Description	Intangibles— All Levels
Level I: Organization makes no real attempt to quantify or address diversity measurement as a key performance factor.	· **Activities Focused Level:** Primarily activities, celebrations, slogans, and other programming that is more "event-based" support of diversity. Performance is measured based upon counts such as attendance, number of events held per year, etc.	· **Activities Focused Level:** Primarily activities, celebrations, slogans, and other programming that is more "event-based" support of diversity. Performance is measured based upon counts such as attendance, number of events held per year, etc.	**All Levels:** Organization consistently demonstrates superior capability in optimizing diverse human capital assets and includes anecdotal as well as quantitative evidence of diversity as a key performance driver
Level II : Organization makes a basic or little attempt to address Diversity Measurement as a key performance factor	· **Compliance Level (compliance based management of metrics):** Representation, Voluntary and Involuntary Turnover reduction, and Litigation Exposure Reduction.	· **Compliance Level (compliance based management of metrics):** Representation, Voluntary and Involuntary Turnover reduction, and Litigation Exposure Reduction.	
Level III: Organization makes cursory, non-systematic attempts to address at least some components of diversity metrics as a key performance factor. At best, the organization demonstrates adequate, or baseline, capability that form a good foundation for improvement in the organization's performance	· **Inclusion Level (loosely defined use and tracking of metrics):** Talent Pipeline Development, Retention, Environment and Culture Improvement, Knowledge Development, Work-life Improvement, Succession Planning, Promotion, Employee Satisfaction, Reasonable Accommodation, Leadership Accountability and Commitment, Diversity Initiatives Achievement, Supplier Diversity, and External Recognition, Human Capital Depletion, Compensation Equity, Employee Network Impact, Utilization Rates, etc.	· **Inclusion Level (loosely defined use and tracking of metrics):** Talent Pipeline Development, Retention, Environment and Culture Improvement, Knowledge Development, Work-life Improvement, Succession Planning, Promotion, Employee Satisfaction, Reasonable Accommodation, Leadership Accountability and Commitment, Diversity Initiatives Achievement, Supplier Diversity, and External Recognition, Human Capital Depletion, Compensation Equity, Employee Network Impact, Utilization Rates, etc.	· **Intangibles Level (anecdotal):** Soft or qualitative measures that cannot be quantified but are important outcomes for the organization.

Rating Level	Profit Focused Description	Government / Non-Profit Description	Intangibles—All Levels
Level IV: Organization is beginning to systematically extend its diversity measurement capability to influence critical performance outcomes and organizational objectives.	· **Strategic Performance Level (strategic performance and scorecard management of metrics)**: Productivity Improvement, Innovation, Creativity, Cycle-time Reduction, Market Share Improvement, Customer Retention and Satisfaction, Human Capital Readiness Level, Human Capital Competence Level, Human Capital Commitment Level, Human Capital Satisfaction Level, Climate Impact, and Cost Level, etc.	· **Strategic Performance Level (strategic performance and scorecard management of metrics)**: Productivity Improvement, Innovation, Creativity, Cycle-time Reduction, Market Share Improvement, Customer Retention and Satisfaction, Human Capital Readiness Level, Human Capital Competence Level, Human Capital Commitment Level, Human Capital Satisfaction Level, Climate Impact, and Cost Level, etc.	**All Levels**: Organization consistently demonstrates superior capability in optimizing diverse human capital assets and includes anecdotal as well as quantitative evidence of diversity as a key performance driver
Level V: Organization consistently demonstrates superior capability in optimizing diverse human capital assets to influence critical performance outcomes and organizational objectives.	· **Profit-Focused ROI Level (ROI management of metrics)**: DROI, BCR	· **Mission Focused ROI Level (ROI management of metrics)**: DROI, BCR	· **Intangibles Level (anecdotal)**: Soft or qualitative measures that cannot be quantified but are important outcomes for the organization.·

The Hubbard Five Level Diversity Analytics and Measurement Taxonom
By Dr. Edward E. Hubbard, Copyright © 2005, All Rights Reserved

Utilizing Diversity ROI Analytics and Measurement is a Strategy Worth Implementing Today and for the Future!

If you want to measure the effects and value of diversity training at any level, you can. You can even put a dollar value on your Diversity training's impact. The approaches discussed here are proof that no matter what type of diversity training intervention has been applied, it can be measured and evaluated. The most important requirement is that you follow the principles and steps described in this and other chapters.

If it were easy to measure diversity training intervention effects, many more people would be doing this as a matter of routine. We must evaluate the ROI of Diversity Training without exception to be regarded as a professional discipline and field of expertise like any other part of the business. True Diversity Professionals recognize that adhering to these practices can determine the level of effectiveness achieved by those affected and the success of the organization. When we start to show management exactly how much value diversity training efforts can contribute to the process of building an inclusive work environment and its performance impact, diversity will be viewed as critical to the organization's performance and results!

References

"Diversity's Business Case Doesn't Add Up" (Fay Hansen, Workforce.com, February, 2009)

"Value of Diversity Training Tough to Measure," (NPR Radio, Talk of the Nation, March 9, 2010, NEAL CONAN, host: NPR.org),

"Who's Still Biased?", Drake Bennett, *Boston Globe*, March, 2010"

Hubbard, Edward E., *How to Calculate Diversity Return on Investment*. California: Global Insights Publishing, 1999.

Hubbard, Edward E., *The Diversity Scorecard: Evaluating the Impact of Diversity on Organizational Performance*. Massachusetts: Butterworth-Heinemann, Elsevier Publishing, 2004.

Hubbard, Edward E., *The Diversity Discipline: Implementing Diversity Work with a Strategy, Structure, and ROI Measurement Focus*. California: Global Insights Publishing, 2009.

Jackson, Susan E., *Diversity in the Workplace*. New York: The Guilford Press, 1992.

Plummer, Deborah L,. *Handbook of Diversity Management*. Maryland: University Press of America, Inc. 2003

Index

A

Activity-Level or Intangibles, 262

ADDIE model, 107, 110

Alignment with Strategy, 49

Analysis, 8, 10, 14, 34, 35, 36, 42, 71, 74, 103, 107, 111, 112, 113, 115, 117, 122, 126, 127, 128, 132, 134, 136, 138, 141, 143, 149, 150, 152, 153, 156, 157, 167, 228, 229, 254

Application and Implementation Objectives, 7, 66, 71

B

Barksdale and Lund, 115, 116, 117, 126, 128, 129, 130, 132, 134, 138, 143, 149

BCR, 44, 222, 223, 224, 270, 273

Benefit/Cost Ratio, 222

Business drivers, 129

Business Needs, 7, 10, 70, 71, 74, 76

C

Calculating the Costs and Benefits, 43

Chain of Impact, 64, 80

Chief Executive Officer, 20

Conditions, 65, 66

Converting the Contribution to Money, 41

Cost Categories, 210

cost of quality, 41

Criteria, 65, 67

critical incident reports, 155

D

Design, 4, 8, 107, 108, 210, 213, 287

Development, 8, 9, 107, 109, 157, 160, 210, 213, 224, 267, 272

Direct Costs, 211

Diversity Alignment Matrix, 132

Diversity Attitude Change, 9, 174

Diversity Knowledge Change, 9, 173

Diversity Needs Analysis, 36, 114, 144, 149, 150, 153

Diversity Return on Investment, 2, 7, 9, 13, 22, 30, 33, 34, 35, 53, 63, 69, 81, 101, 105, 156, 157, 204, 207, 208, 219, 254, 261, 268, 269, 275

Diversity Role Play Checklist, 9, 182

diversity scorecard, 46

Diversity Self-Assessment, 9, 178

Diversity Skill (Behavior) Change, 173

Diversity Training Return on Investment, 12, 13, 14, 21, 22, 37, 52, 156

Donald Kirkpatrick, 103

DROI, 7, 9, 14, 22, 26, 29, 33, 34, 35, 36, 37, 39, 40, 41, 42, 43, 44, 48, 50, 52, 55, 63, 69, 71, 74, 81, 104, 105, 123, 145, 147, 151, 156, 207, 208, 211, 215, 216, 219, 220, 221, 223, 224, 225, 226, 227, 228, 229, 240, 245, 246, 247, 248, 249, 251, 261, 268, 269, 270, 271, 273

DROI®, 69

DTROI©, 12, 13, 21, 22, 37, 52, 56, 60, 64, 112, 137, 144, 227, 228, 229, 233, 249, 252, 257

The Author

Dr. Edward E. Hubbard is President and CEO of Hubbard & Hubbard, Inc., Petaluma, CA, an international organization and human performance-consulting corporation that specializes in techniques for applied business performance improvement, workforce diversity measurement, instructional design and organizational development.

He is the founder of the Hubbard Diversity Measurement and Productivity Institute and is also author of more than 40 books including the groundbreaking books: *Measuring Diversity Results, How to Calculate Diversity Return-on-Investment, Pathways to Diversity Metrics for Corporate Legal and Law Firms, The Diversity Scorecard, Implementing Diversity Measurement and Management,* and the *Manager's Pocket Guide to Diversity Management.*

Dr. Hubbard is one of the first metrics authors in the field of diversity. As a result of his extensive research in the area of diversity measurement and expertise in computer programming, he is one of the first to develop automated software technologies for measuring diversity return-on-investment and performance improvements.

He has performed client work in organizational change and diverse workforce integration for private Fortune 500 companies, the U.S. Government, and corporate clients in the Far East, the Netherlands, other parts of Europe, Hawaii, Samoa, and locations throughout the Pacific Rim and the Federated States of Micronesia. His work includes assisting organizations with issues such as diverse workforce integration, staff development, quality improvement, performance improvement strategies, and restructuring work teams to utilize the strengths of a multiethnic workforce. Additionally, work in these countries include strategic planning and analysis, workforce recruitment and retention strategies, diversity return-on-investment metrics and methods, succession planning and development, as well as full scale organization development interventions.

Dr. Hubbard is an internationally known and respected business consultant, trainer, former professor and Director at Ohio State University, a business professional at several Fortune 100 corporations, such as Computer Systems Analyst, Xerox Corporation and the Informatics Corporation, Computer Room Operations Manager, Battelle Memorial Institute, Internal Consultant and Education Specialist, Mead Corporation, and Corporate Director, Training, Organization Development and Compensation for the 17-billion-dollar McKesson Corporation.

The July/August 2007 Issue of *Profiles in Diversity Journal* featured Dr. Hubbard as the "Diversity Pioneer" in Diversity Metrics and Measurement. The American Society for Training and Development (ASTD) inducted Dr. Ed Hubbard into the prestigious "ASTD New Guard for 2003." The New Guard represents selected "members of the Training and Development profession who are taking themselves and the field in new directions." He serves as a Editorial Advisory Board member of *Harvard Business Review* and *Diversity Executive* magazines and has served as a member of the ASTD ROI Advisory Board. In addition, Dr. Hubbard received double honors being named to the prestigious Who's Who in Leading American Executives and Who's Who Worldwide of Global Business Leaders. Memberships are limited to those individuals who have demonstrated outstanding leadership and achievement in their occupation, industry or profession. Some of Dr. Hubbard's other book titles include: *The Hidden Side of Employee Resistance To Change, Managing Customer Service on the Frontline, Managing Your Business For Profitable Growth, Hiring Strategies For Long-Term Success, How To Start Your Own Business With Empty Pockets, Managing Organizational Change: Strategies For Building Commitment.* Dr. Hubbard serves on the Advisory Board for *Diversity Executive* Magazine and serves on the *Harvard Business Review* Advisory Council.

Articles by Dr. Hubbard have appeared in magazines and newspapers such as *Inc. Magazine, Fortune, Forbes, Cultural Diversity at Work, American Society for Training and Development Journal, Society for Human Resources Management* (SHRM) *HR Magazine, Sonoma Business Magazine, Organization Development Network Journal, The Cleveland Plain Dealer, Strategic Diversity & Inclusion Management* (SDIM) magazine (where he serves as a Board Member), *The Diversity Factor Magazine, DiversityInc.,* and many others. He has also been featured in several business films and management development videos, on radio programs, and is a regularly featured speaker, and keynote for national and international conferences, tele-conferences, seminars, and workshops. A brief list of Hubbard & Hubbard, Inc. clients include Prudential Financial, Starbucks, Inc., McDonalds Corporation, M.D. Anderson Cancer Center, Kaiser Permanente, America Online, working with key Military leaders at the Pentagon, U.S. and abroad, and many others.

Dr. Hubbard is an expert in Organizational Behavior, Organizational Analysis, Applied Performance Improvement and Measurement Strategies, Strategic Planning, Diversity Measurement and Analytics, and Organizational Change Methodologies.

Dr. Hubbard earned Bachelors and Masters Degrees from Ohio State University and earned a Ph.D. with Honors in Business Administration.

Books by Dr. Edward E. Hubbard

MEASURING DIVERSITY RESULTS

gives you a reliable, work-tested system of data collection and diversity and productivity measurement tools that will feed back the organization's progress through solid, factual results. In this ground-breaking book, Dr. Hubbard takes you through the mechanics of creating simple mathematical formulas and advanced calculations and approaches for measuring the efficiency and effectiveness of key Diversity change efforts.

Cost: $ 34.95   Order# HH-1-883733-17-0   Book & Software COMBO: $ 149.00

HOW TO CALCULATE DIVERSITY RETURN ON INVESTMENT

is a timely and cutting edge book that enhances on Dr. Hubbard's earlier book Measuring Diversity Results. In this book, he helps you demonstrate diversity's link to dollar ROI in a step-by-step format that is easy to apply. You are provided with a concrete road map with detailed instructions to design, measure, analyze, and/or improve diversity initiatives' impact and demonstrate its financial return on investment.

Cost: $ 42.95   Order# HH-1-883733-21-9

THE DIVERSITY SCORECARD: Evaluating the Impact of Diversity on Organizational Performance

This book by Dr. Edward Hubbard demonstrates his continued commitment to the field of diversity and ROI. It is designed to provide step-by-step instructions, worksheets and examples to help diversity executives and managers analyze and track the impact of their diversity initiatives to mobilize the organization for strategic culture change. Diversity professionals know they must begin to show how diversity is linked to the bottom-line in hard numbers or they will have difficulty maintaining funds, gaining support, and obtaining resources to generate progress.

The Diversity Scorecard focuses on tools and techniques to make sure diversity professionals collect the right type of data that will help ensure the organization's success both now and in the future. To further your learning, Dr. Hubbard has created the Diversity Measurement & Productivity Institute (DM&P) which offers regularly scheduled workshops that are built around the skills and techniques provided in his various research-based books.

Cost: $39.99   Order# BH-0-7506-7457-1   Book & Software COMBO: $410.00

IMPLEMENTING DIVERSITY MEASUREMENT AND MANAGEMENT

Casebook Volume 1 of the Diversity in Practice series edited by Dr. Edward Hubbard shows case after case of diversity professionals highlighting how their work in diversity is making a significant difference and financial impact on organization's performance. This 400-page book is divided into two parts. Part one concentrates on diversity measurement applications which demonstrates diversity's financial impact. Part two highlights the practical approaches in diversity management that build strategic capability for the organization. If you are interested in being recognized for your work in diversity by writing a case, contact Hubbard & Hubbard, Inc. we welcome your contribution to the field of diversity

Cost: $ 44.95   Order# HH-1-883733-24-3

THE MANAGER'S POCKET GUIDE TO DIVERSITY MANAGEMENT

is designed to help you build diversity management skills to create a high performing work environment. It is meant be used as an interactive workbook to test your skills, teach or reinforce diversity concepts, and provide techniques to utilize a diverse workforce to improve organizational performance.

Cost: $ 14.95   Item# HRD-MPGDM

THE DIVERSITY DISCIPLINE: IMPLEMENTING DIVERSITY WORK WITH A STRATEGY, STRUCTURE, AND ROI MEASUREMENT FOCUS

is a timely and cutting edge book that enhances on Dr. Hubbard's earlier book How to Calculate Diversity Return On Investment. In this book, he helps you demonstrate diversity's link to dollar ROI in a step-by-step format that is easy to apply. You are provided with a concrete road map with detailed instructions to design, measure, analyze, and/or improve diversity initiatives' impact and demonstrate its financial return on investment.

Cost: $ 42.95   Order# HH-1-883733-27-8

DIVERSITY PERFORMANCE CONSULTING

Providing diversity professionals with a strategic step-by-step diversity consulting process. Publication scheduled for late 2011.

Cost: $ 44.95   Order# HH-1-883733-28-6

A Sampling of Tools and Services from Hubbard and Hubbard, Inc.

DIVERSITY INSIGHTS PROFILE

The workplace is changing to reflect a highly diverse workforce. To be effective, organizations and their employees must be able to understand, accept, and capitalize on differences. The Diversity Insights Profile® provides a safe, confidential way for employees to explore complex diversity issues and their perceptions across two key dimensions: Diversity Comprehension and Behavioral Performance.

This research-based assessment instrument is a self-scoring tool which helps employees examine their perceptions and "cultural programming" to provide "insight" into their current level of knowledge and skill when interacting with people who are different than themselves. It is designed for organizations and individuals interested in developing and/or improving interpersonal interactions.

It contains interpretation and analysis to help employees calculate and summarize the impact of their responses as well provides detailed Action Planning worksheets for improvement. The feedback resulting from this instrument will increase awareness of individual, ethnic, and cultural differences and identify potential areas for improvement. Spanish Version also available.

Cost: 5-Pak $69.95   Order# HH-DIP-5PK

Although interest in measuring the effects of diversity has been growing, the topic still challenges even the most sophisticated and progressive diversity departments. Managers know they must begin to show how diversity is linked to the bottom-line or they will have difficulty maintaining funding, gaining support, and assessing progress. The **Hubbard Diversity Measurement & Productivity Institute** (HDM&P) provides on-going, solution-based skill building with a focus on measuring organizational productivity and results.

HUBBARD
Diversity ROI
INSTITUTE

The Hubbard Diversity ROI Institute is the leading resource on Diversity ROI Analytics Research, Consulting, Training, and Networking for practitioners of the Hubbard Diversity ROI Methodology® (DROI®)

The Hubbard Diversity ROI (DROI®) Institute — An applied sciences organization dedicated to the development of processes and methods that demonstrate Diversity's measurable value and performance improvement impact on an organization's bottom-line. We provide Diversity ROI Analytics research, consulting, benchmarking, publications and online analytical services and tools utilizing the Hubbard Diversity ROI Methodology® (DROI®).

Hubbard & Hubbard, Inc.

Hubbard & Hubbard, Inc., has created and distributes several Easy-to-Use automated measurement products and software systems that put the power of measurement technology at your fingertips!

MetricLINK® A Comprehensive Performance Measurement & Management System for Organizational Excellence The MetricLINK® measurement system is extremely flexible and can be used in a wide variety of applications. It can be used to Design, Measure, Manage, Report, and Track Measures in a wide variety of industries and can be applied in uses such as...

Private Industry	Government	Non-Profit	Community
Balanced Scorecard Statistics	Balanced Scorecard Statistics	Healthcare Statistics	Volunteerism Scorecard Statistics
Quality Scorecard Statistics	Quality Scorecard Statistics	Patient Care Statistics	Community Impact Statistics
Team Performance Statistics	Team Performance Statistics	Team Performance Statistics	Donation & Philanthropy Statistics
Diversity Scorecard	Diversity Scorecard	Diversity Scorecard	Diversity Scorecard
Six Sigma Metrics	Six Sigma Metrics	Six Sigma Metrics	Safety Statistics
Human Resources Scorecard	Human Resources Scorecard	Human Resources Scorecard	Six Sigma Metrics
Process Management Scorecard	Process Management Scorecard	Productivity Improvement Statistics	Productivity Improvement Statistics
Organizational Effectiveness & Efficiency Statistics	Organizational Effectiveness Efficiency Statistics	Donation & Philanthropy Statistics	Organizational Effectiveness & Efficiency Statistics
Productivity Improvement Statistics	Safety Statistics	Student Performance Metrics	Safety Statistics
Manufacturing Statistics	Customer Satisfaction Statistics	Customer Satisfaction Statistics	Process Management Scorecard

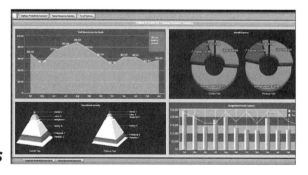

Hubbard MetricLink® Gold and Platinum: Dashboard and Scorecard Reporting Services

"A State-of-the-Art Online Measurement Service that is Redefining Diversity ROI Analytics and Business Impact Reporting" **MetricLINK®** offers *two powerful online Diversity Analytics services* that help you reduce the time it takes to calculate, track, analyze and report your diversity initiatives' ROI (DROI) performance impact in financial and non-financial terms!

Hubbard & Hubbard, Inc., offers standardized and custom diversity measurement services, including:

- Diversity Scorecards
  building strategic measurement tools for reporting the impact of your diversity initiatives

- Diversity Initiative
  Impact/ROI Analysis
  calculating the financial impact of your diversity initiatives

- Diversity Dashboards
  creating interactive, graphic displays of your diversity ROI result

- Diversity Culture and
  Systems Audits
  assessing the diversity climate and culture

- Diverse Work Team
  Impact Analysis
  analyzing the effectiveness of your diverse work teams

- Global Diversity Metrics
  providing a numerical breakdown of your world-wide diversity initiatives' impact

- Diversity Council Impact Analysis
  assessing the effectiveness of your diversity council

- Diversity Strategic
  Planning Development
  creating a strategic plan for implementing your company's diversity goals

- DROI™ Analytics™
  creating a strategic diversity measurement framework for assessing and benchmarking your diversity progress